Carol Spe

Style Directions for Men

PIATKUS

I dedicate this book to the other man in my life, Sam, a truly unique individual . . . *but please read the section on socks!*

First published in 1999 by
Judy Piatkus (Publishers) Ltd.,
5 Windmill Street, London W1T 2JA

This paperback edition published in 2001

A catalogue record for this book is available from the British Library

ISBN 0 7499 1865 9 hbk
ISBN 0 7499 2094 7 pbk

Designed by Jerry Goldie
Data capture and manipulation by
Create Publishing Services, Bath
Printed and bound in Great Britain by
Bath Press (Glasgow) PLC

Acknowledgements

My heartfelt thanks to all the following individuals and companies who have enthusiastically supplied advice, pictures or their talents for this book:

Piatkus Books – Judy Piatkus, Philip Cotterell, Gill Bailey and especially Rachel Winning whose frantic messages on my ansaphone I will miss terribly.

Margaret Bateman – my amazing secretary who after six years, six books and 10,000 Mail-Order-Makeovers is still going strong! (Tele: 01223 812737)

Jerry Goldie – for the fantastic design and layout of this book – and his extreme calm and patience at all times. (Tele: 020 8891 4886)

Hilary Kidd (a.k.a Willy) – for the beautiful illustrations which she somehow deciphered from my efforts. (Tele: 01768 895088)

Amway (UK) – Jean-François Heurtas, Sharon and Andy Norman, Caroline Porter and Sharon Harrison for their enthusiastic support of my Style Directions concept and for skin and hair care information and pictures in Chapter 5. A great company to work with. (Tele: 01908 363000)

Clynol – for the many hairstyle pictures featured in this book and the loan of top UK hairdresser, Paul Falltrick, and his assistant Jenny Pringle, for the fantastic hair makeovers in Chapter 8. (Tele: 01708 442266)

Tony Chau – photographer extraordinaire for his talents and good humour on our photo-shoot for Chapter 8 (he got the dates right this time!) (Tele: 020 7241 4810)

House of Fraser – for supplying the majority of the fashion photos in this book – especially Dan Harper in the press office for all his help and on-going support. (Tele: 020 7963 2590)

Debenhams – for other fashion photos throughout this book. (Tele: 020 7408 3827)

T.M. Lewin & Sons of Jermyn Street, London – for the beautiful shirt and tie pictures in Chapter 7. (Tele: 020 7839 1664)

Hackett of Sloane Street, London – for leather goods and accessories pictures in Chapter 7. (Tele: 020 7730 3331)

High & Mighty – outfitters for big and tall men, for pictures featured in Chapter 3. (Tele: 01488 684666)

The Holding Company of Kings Road, London – for pictures of clothing storage facilities in Chapter 6. (Tele: 020 7420 1700)

Boots Opticians – for the wonderful array of glasses featured in Chapter 2. (Tele: 0121 236 9501)

Dulux Paints – for the room-décor pictures in Chapter 4. (Tele: 020 7950 2869)

Bally – for supplying a fantastic range of footwear for Chapter 8. (Tele: 020 7287 2266)

Makeover Volunteers – last, but definitely not least, an extra special thank you to all the brave men who took part in our makeover days for Chapter 8 – great sports who really made my job so enjoyable.

Note – the exact merchandise/service featured in this book may not be available at the date you purchase and read the book. Please contact the above companies for details of their current ranges. All colours are subject to the limitations of the printing process.

Chapter 1

Image Directions

Above: More and more men today are realizing the potential of the 'look good, feel good' factor.

Something has happened to men over the last decade. When I began my business in the early 1990s, my customers for image, colour and style advice were 99 per cent women. The odd men (and I mean that in the nicest possible way!) who comprised the remaining 1 per cent, were usually husbands or boyfriends of my female customers who were dragged along reluctantly to receive my advice – usually for the benefit of the woman who invariably bought all his clothes. Also at this time, over 80 per cent of men's clothing in one of Britain's leading high street retailers was bought by women; for underwear, the figure rose to over 90 per cent. Not so long ago, then, men's interest in shopping appeared to be nil!

Other clients for men's image consultations came from the corporate sector as businesses slowly came to realize during the 1980s that the appearance of their employees was just as important as the image of their products, brochures, advertising and office décor. This work, however, mainly comprised giving executives advice on the colour and style of their suits, shirts and ties, with only occasional references to casual, leisure, weekend or holiday wear. The aim of such seminars or consultations was always to give men advice on their most professional or authoritative look in order to enhance their own career and the company's image. As a man, taking an interest in your appearance was, therefore, something forced upon you by your wife, girlfriend or boss.

Men's Liberation

But oh, how things have changed! Just take a look at the number of men's magazines fighting for space with the women's titles in the newsagents and bookshops. Ten years ago, sales of men's magazines were very low in comparison to those for women, and the magazines were in any case devoted to a particular hobby or sport: golf, sailing, football, DIY, cars (not forgetting, of course, the 'girlie mags' in the plain wrappers on the top shelf!). Only *Esquire* existed for men interested in style, fashion and grooming, but its market was predominantly composed of affluent male executives and this was reflected in its advertisements for designer clothes, accessories and expensive cars.

Today the competition between men's magazines is fierce with titles such as *GQ*, *Men's Health*, *Loaded* and *FHM* (to name but a few) joining the older *Esquire* and *Arena* in a huge circulation war. The poaching of editors, writers, photographers and other talents is as rife as within the women's market, and the army of male models and the fees they can command grows stronger every day. The content of these magazines has a lot in common with women's magazines – articles on fashion, grooming, fitness, food and the topic which sells all magazines, sex. There is perhaps a little more space devoted to cars and sports in men's magazines, but the close parallels between the female and male magazine markets were undreamed of a decade ago.

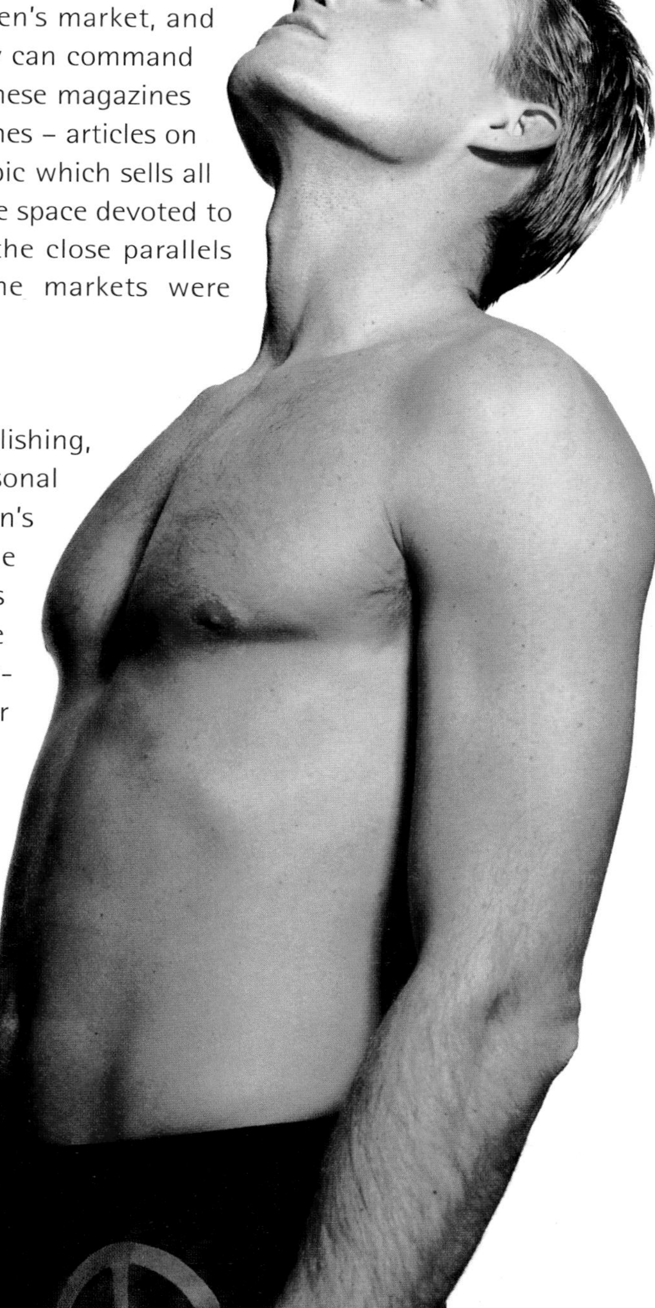

Below: Today men are spending more money than ever before on grooming products and routines.

Face Up to It

Not only is business booming in men's publishing, but the fastest-growing sector of the 'personal care and toiletries' market is the area of men's grooming products. Back in the 1950s the only male item in the bathroom cabinet was a pot of Brylcreem. This was joined in the 1960s by a very daring companion, after-shave (splash it on all over), which, together with socks and handkerchiefs, became the favourite Christmas present of wives and girlfriends for several decades. Today, men virtually need a bathroom cabinet of their own to accommodate the array of moisturizers, scuffing lotions, toners, hair gels, hair volumizers and so forth which are sold in their billions each year. Buying a present for a man these days is as confusing as buying for your mother – bring back the days of socks and hankies!

On Your Back

The growth of the men's toiletries market has been steadily increasing over the 1990s, but the one area which seems to have exploded out of nowhere is the rise of salon treatments for men. Not only are men at it standing up in the bathroom, but they are also taking it lying down in the salon! As more and more men are signing up to join gyms and health clubs and opening fashion accounts at department stores, the establishments concerned are taking the opportunity to open up Men's Grooming Studios (definitely not Beauty Salons!) to offer services on their premises which, until a few years ago, no self-respecting male would ever have considered. Listed below are just some of the treatments offered at a leading London department store – and, it is always fully booked!

Men's Grooming Studio

Facials

- Mini prescription
- Full prescription
- Anti-ageing
- Refining, deep cleanse
- Stress (incorporating neck massage)
- Eye – de-stress, moisture, firm

Manicure and Pedicure

- Hands only
- Feet only
- Pedicure with half leg massage
- Hands with paraffin wax (for softening)
- Feet with paraffin wax (for softening)

Waxing (for hair removal)

- Brows
- Face
- Back and shoulders
- Chest
- Abdomen
- Chest and abdomen
- Half leg
- Full leg and brief line (ouch!)
- Lower back and buttocks*

Body

- Self-tan application (face and body)
- Deep cleanse of back

* Carol recommends this treatment for all builders!

The Peacock Principle

Left: Martin Kemp expresses his peacock potential in the 1980s

So why have men suddenly become interested in style, grooming and fashion? Why are they now prepared to spend time and money on their clothes, magazines and toiletries rather than leave it to the women? Recent research by one of the leading men's magazines found that 75 per cent of its readers not only shop for their own clothes now, but actually enjoy it! Young men, teenagers in particular, spend entire Saturdays in a shopping mall when once they would only go there under duress. At the time of writing, a major magazine publisher is putting the finishing touches to the first magazine aimed at teenage boys. It will be packed with features on fashion, grooming, pop music, sport (and, undoubtedly, sex) – in other words, a complete parallel to the magazines for teenage girls which have sold in their hundreds of thousands each week since the 1960s.

The reason for this surge in interest in all matters sartorial lies in the fact that men have always been the peacocks of the human species. The desire to look and feel attractive is nothing new – it's just gone underground within Western culture for a few decades. You need only think back to the appearance and dress of men in past eras – the Elizabethans in their silk doublets, hose, ruff and codpieces, or the Regency dandies in their tight-waisted cutaway coats, lace ruffles and oversize top hats. Fashion, perfume, posing and pampering were part and parcel of many men's lives until the Victorian era, when prudish attitudes and values decreed such matters unmanly and ungodly.

During the first half of the twentieth century, men's appearance and behaviour remained quite sober – any departure by a man into the areas of fashion, perfume, jewellery or even colour were regarded as signs of homosexuality, for which he was ridiculed or rejected. I shall never forget persuading my father to buy his first brightly coloured shirt in the 1960s (it was orange nylon!), which resulted in an older uncle in the family (who had very strait-laced Victorian attitudes) refusing to let us into his house. It obviously didn't help that my sister and I, who were both teenagers at the time, were sporting mini-skirts, white boots and several layers of false eyelashes!

It's Reigning Men

So men are finally back on their thrones as the reigning monarchs of style and panache. Mind you, it has taken quite a long time, and with quite a few setbacks and disastrous style-decades in the process.

- The 1920s and 1930s made quite modest advances – plus-four trousers, Argyle checks and silk cravats.
- The 1940s were the war years, and sobriety returned once more as society was forced to become more serious and sensible.
- The 1950s are cited by many as the real beginnings of the return of 'peacock power'. Young Teddy Boys strutted their stuff in frock coats and cockscombed hair – very reminiscent of the Regency dandies.
- The 1960s saw the return of colour to the male wardrobe (hence my dad's orange nylon shirt), which reached its zenith in the heady days of 'Flower Power' when men were not even afraid to wear a cow-bell necklace or a daffodil behind the ear.
- The 1970s are often described as 'the decade that style forgot' – satin suits, platform shoes, permed hair, medal-

The 1960s (above) saw the return of colour and pattern to men's wardrobes, while the 1980s saw the beginnings of hair colour and make-up for men (right).

lions and, for the first time in many decades, make-up on men – (albeit they were mostly pop stars). International rock stars such as David Bowie and Marc Bolan made it OK once and for all for men to enjoy dressing-up and having as much fun as the girls with fashion and changing images.

- The 1980s saw the continuation of the dressing-up theme with the New Romantics – frilly pirate shirts, hoop earrings, leather trousers and ponytails. This decade, however, also saw the emergence of several other fashion looks determined by lifestyle – the punk, the yuppie and, later in the decade, the anti-fashion look called grunge which signalled the fact that men had made their point about their 'feminine' side and were ready to adopt more realistic and practical modes of dress.
- The 1990s, the age of the individual, saw men finally achieve image freedom after decades of mainly being pressurized into just one or two looks. As a new millennium begins, men have a huge variety of styles and colours to choose from. Rather than being a square peg in a round hole, you can now choose the best garments for your individual shape, colouring, age and lifestyle. Rather than feeling that you look an idiot (as may have happened in past decades), today you can be sure that on all occasions you are looking and feeling your very best.

Look Good, Feel Good

Men have also come to realize a fact that women have known for a long time – that paying attention to one's appearance can pay dividends in the long term in terms of self-assurance and self-respect. Even small changes such as new glasses or more fashionable shoes can affect other people's perceptions of you, which in turn affects your own confidence and self-esteem. This can be viewed as a kind of circle of success, in which looking good is the starting point of an on-going journey of confidence-building and self-discovery.

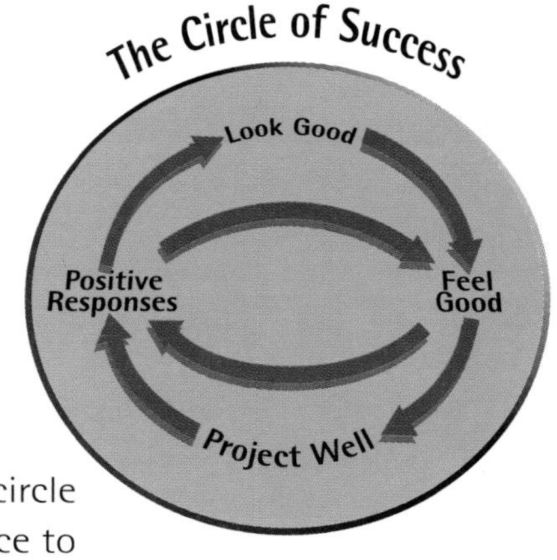

When you look good and know it, the resulting feel-good factor enables you to project yourself with more conviction and authority. This will induce positive responses from family, friends, colleagues and strangers, which simply adds to your feel-good factor and keeps the circle in motion. Positive responses also give you added confidence to make more changes to your appearance thus magnifying the circle's effects still further.

The famous American research into the power of appearance by Professor Mehrabian proved that 55 per cent of someone's opinion of us is based on our appearance – height, weight, colouring, clothing, hairstyle and accessories such as watches, pens, cases and bags. So getting all these things right counts for more than half of the total impression we make. The next 38 per cent relates to how we present ourselves – body language, eye contact, confidence and so on. So, if you know your appearance is good, the chances are that your 38 per cent will be pretty impressive too. This leaves 7 per cent for what you actually know or say in any given situation.

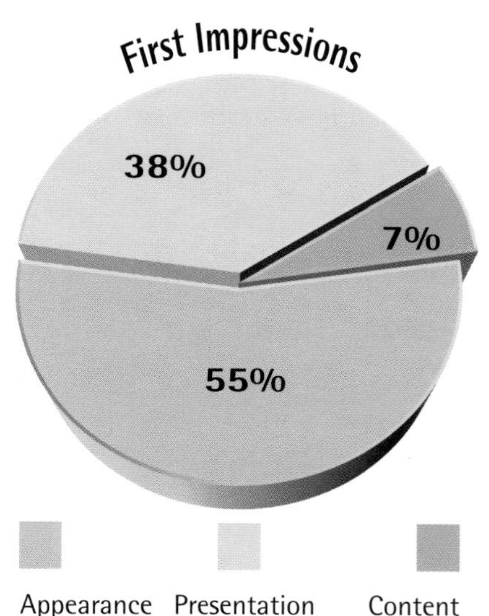

Our appearance is therefore a means of non-verbal communication – a method of giving people information about ourselves which causes them to form opinions about us on a conscious (and sometimes subconscious) level. By changing just small aspects of our appearance – colours, hairstyle, glasses – we can change people's reaction to us even on a day-to-day basis, and so achieve the desired response whatever the circumstances.

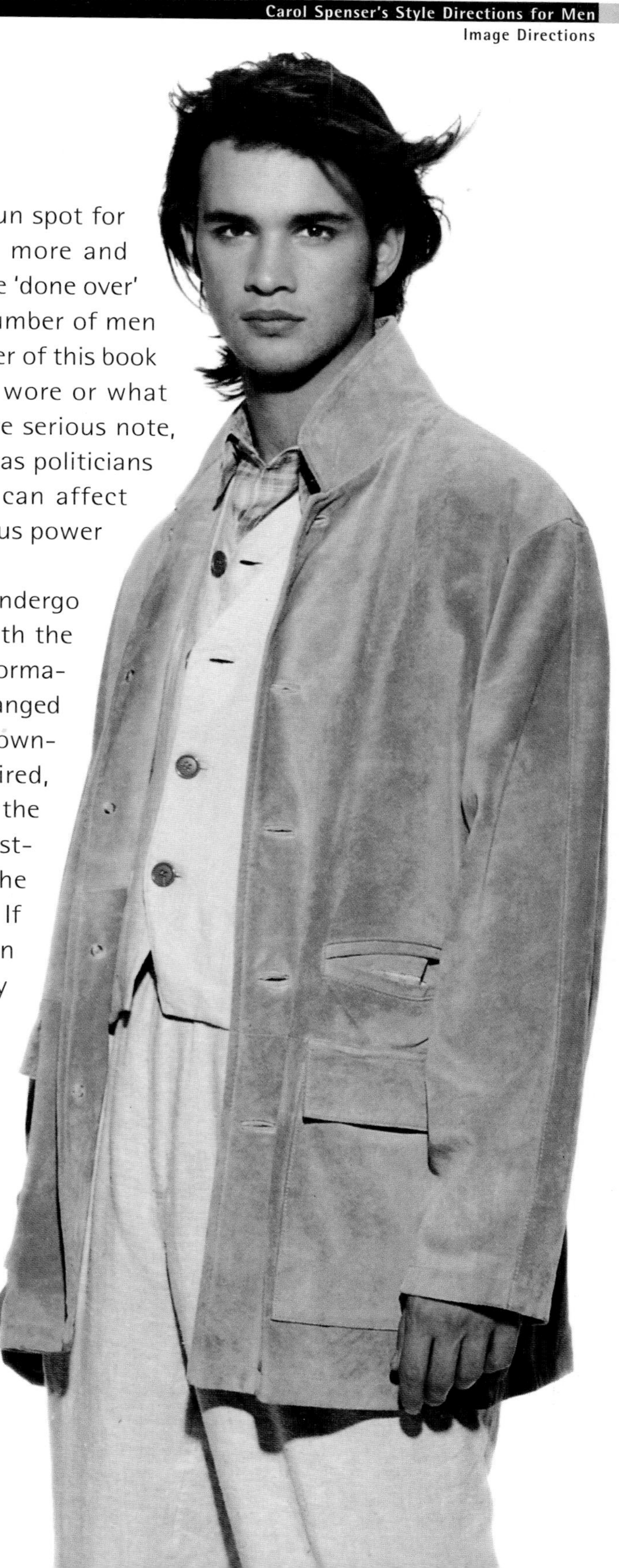

Makeover Magic

Changing someone's image can be a fun spot for a TV show or magazine feature, and more and more men are writing to me asking to be 'done over' for the media. (I was amazed at the number of men who volunteered to be in the last chapter of this book and had no qualms about what they wore or what colour their hair ended up!) On a more serious note, however, men in the public eye - such as politicians - have also realized how their looks can affect public response and give them enormous power on the world stage.

Even an entire political party can undergo a makeover to enhance its standing with the electorate. Think of the amazing transformation of the British Labour Party. It has changed its image from that of the party of the down-trodden working man led by long-haired, donkey jacket-wearing Michael Foot in the 1970s to that of a sophisticated, post-modern, New Age party led by the bespoke-tailored Tony Blair in the 1990s. If it is true that you are what you wear, then by considering what you wear, as Tony Blair certainly proved with the Labour Party, you can change who you are (in the eye of the perceiver at least!).

Live Your Own Life

The everyday lives of men and women have changed enormously over recent years. There are now many more women in the workforce and an increasing number at extremely

Right: Your chosen hairstyle, clothing, colours and accessories are a means of non-verbal communication, sending out messsages about yourself.

The image of the British Labour Party was changed dramatically in the eyes of the public by a complete change of image of those representing it – especially the leadership. Compare Michael Foot (above) leader in the 1970s to Tony Blair (right) leader in the 1990s.

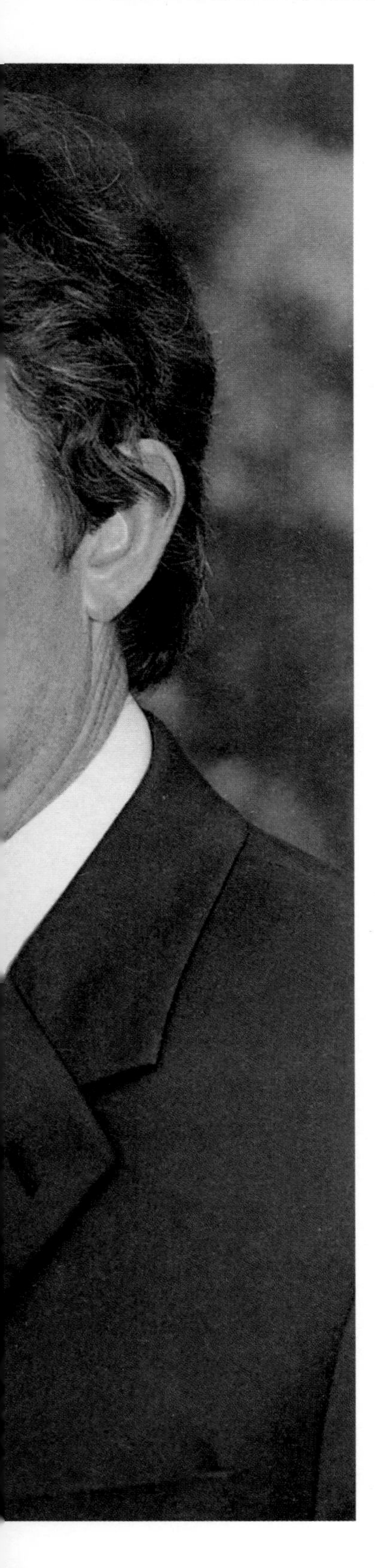

high levels. Men no longer feel it necessary to be the main breadwinner and some, in fact, choose to stay at home in the child-caring role. Working from home, for individuals or couples, is a rapidly increasing trend facilitated by the huge advances in communications technology. Health and fitness is acquiring as much importance in people's lives as their job or status, and leisure/social activities are becoming more valued as lifestyles become more complicated.

In past decades, you had one life at a time. You were a student, or a parent, or a highly paid office worker, or a lowly paid charity worker, and you dressed according to your role in life. Today, you can be all those things at once – a parent who also works full-time in an office, studies at evening classes and does charitable work at weekends. Life is definitely more interesting and varied today, but because we all juggle so many different roles we need a wardrobe which takes us effortlessly from one situation to another. This does not mean we need a vast amount of clothes, but such a wardrobe needs knowledge and planning to provide all the essentials for an early visit to the gym; a morning working at home; an afternoon at the city office; an evening out socializing; and a weekend with the kids. Most people have far too many clothes and yet still end up wearing the same things day after day. The fact of the matter is that they have the wrong clothes for the type of life they now lead, and should reassess their needs.

Get Sorted!

Choosing to sort out your appearance can therefore be prompted by a variety of different reasons:

- To feel more confident (and therefore happier)
- To improve relationships (at home or work)
- To begin a new phase of your life (e.g. from student to worker)
- To get out of a time warp (still stuck in the 1980s?)
- To reflect the different roles of your lifestyle (assess what they are)
- To become more attractive (should that have been top of the list?)

Do you need a change of direction?

Answer the questions in the quiz below to see how much in need of change you are!

Although such quizzes can be viewed as a bit of harmless fun not to be taken too seriously, if you answer them truthfully the results can provide that much needed 'kick in the butt' to precipitate some action.

1. Do you ever receive compliments? ☐ Yes ☐ No
2. Do you always feel you look good? ☐ Yes ☐ No
3. Do you have the right clothes for all occasions? ☐ Yes ☐ No
4. Do you regularly update your look ? ☐ Yes ☐ No
5. Do you keep in touch with trends in fashion, music etc? ☐ Yes ☐ No
6. Do you ever get taken for younger than you are? ☐ Yes ☐ No
7. Do you ever try new fashion colours/styles? ☐ Yes ☐ No
8. Do you have a regular grooming routine? ☐ Yes ☐ No
9. Do you look much different than you did ten years ago? ☐ Yes ☐ No
10. Does your appearance reflect the 'real' you? ☐ Yes ☐ No
11. Do you often envy other men's style and confidence? ☐ Yes ☐ No
12. Do you try to copy others' style without success? ☐ Yes ☐ No
13. Do you make resolutions to change but never do? ☐ Yes ☐ No
14. Do you use clothing to 'hide behind'? ☐ Yes ☐ No
15. Do you feel guilty spending time/money on yourself? ☐ Yes ☐ No

16 Do you lack confidence because of your appearance? ☐ Yes ☐ No

17. Do you have problems selecting items when shopping? ☐ Yes ☐ No
18. Do you want to make more impact at home/work/socially? ☐ Yes ☐ No
19. Do you feel you are 'beyond help'? ☐ Yes ☐ No
20. Do you want to 'get sorted' but don't know where to start? ☐ Yes ☐ No

Your Answers to the Quiz.

If you answered mostly 'No' to questions 1–10 and mostly 'Yes' to questions 11–20, you are in serious need of an overhaul and should start without delay. Your looks, confidence and self-esteem appear to be far lower than they should be and you should take positive steps to remedy the situation. You've nothing to loose and the only way is up!

If your answers were a mixture of 'Yes' and 'No' at random throughout the quiz, you appear to be halfway to a successful image – some days getting it right, some days getting it wrong – but probably with no real idea why it works on some days but not others. A clear understanding of the secret of your best style will have you looking and feeling good 100 per cent of the time.

If you answered mostly 'Yes' to questions 1–10 and mostly 'No' to questions 11–20, you appear to have an appearance and level of self-confidence and esteem which many would envy. As well as my regular TV and magazine makeovers, to date I have also given advice to over twenty thousand individuals via my mail-order makeover service (see P.158 for details), and my heart always sinks when I receive an application and photos from someone (probably like you) who already looks fantastic! I feel my advice will be obvious to the applicant, but I am always pleasantly surprised to receive letters back thanking me for explaining why they were getting things right – for them it was an 'accident' or a natural gift, rather than knowledge. Or perhaps you're a style guru and this book is joining a shelf full of others on similar topics – if so, I hope you enjoy adding to your knowledge in this ever-developing field of men's image and style.

The Right Direction

So whether you're in need of a complete overhaul, just require a little fine-tuning in certain areas, or simply want to add to your knowledge, this book will take you step-by-step in the right direction. By the end of the book, you will be able to:

- Define your facelines and know how to choose your best glasses, hairstyle and necklines
- Re-evaluate your body (its good and not-so-good bits!) and select appropriate garments
- Understand your colouring and see how different colours can project you in a different light
- Follow quick-and-easy grooming routines to keep your face and hair in superb condition
- Begin to plan a wardrobe that caters for your lifestyle needs and budget

If you make any drastic changes as a result of this book, send me a photo!

Chapter 2

Face Directions

Your face is the focal point of your whole appearance. When someone meets you for the first time, in either a business or social situation, they look at your face first and then, without realizing it, their eye travels rapidly up and down your body until it settles on your face again, where eye contact is usually maintained. Your face and everything which surrounds it – hair, glasses, collar, tie and so on – therefore make an extremely important contribution to that crucial 55 per cent of a viewer's opinion of you.

Above: Your face and everything which surrounds it – hair, glasses, neckline – is the focal point of your appearance and a large contributor to the impact you make on others.

Because there is not such a huge choice in fashions and colours for men as there is for women, and because there are not huge differences in the shapes of men's bodies as there are among women's, a man's face, together with his choice of hairstyle, glasses, shirt and tie, becomes one of the key ways for him to express some degree of personality and individuality. Your face is a unique asset: your body or cut of suit may be the same as the next man's but your face is as individual as your fingerprints. You only need to look around an office where men are required to wear a 'uniform' suit of navy or grey (or look along the benches of the Houses of Parliament!) to see what signals the differences between the men present – without a doubt, it is their choice of hairstyles, glasses, shirts and ties.

The face has often been called 'the window to the soul' because it says so much about who you are. For the same reason people also talk about 'reading a face like a book'. But as your life changes and your personality, career or lifestyle develop in different ways, you need to keep reassessing that message. Hanging on to the same hairstyle, glasses, type of collar and pattern of tie you had in your twenties is rarely appropriate or flattering when you are in your forties or fifties – in fact, it can turn you into a figure of ridicule.

Having a 1970s collar-curling hairstyle or 1980s brightly framed, owl-like glasses indicates either a sad attempt to hold on to one's youth or complete unawareness of contemporary moods and culture. The latter situation is actually quite serious: research has shown that men who look old-fashioned are often regarded as also being outdated in their knowledge, abilities and attitudes. At work, of course, this can have profound effects; those with a more 'current' or 'contemporary' look are selected at interviews or for promotion, while those with the 'dinosaur demeanour' are often passed over.

Defining Your Face

To work out how to choose your most complimentary hairstyle, glasses, collar, ties and other necklines, there are two aspects of your face which you need to understand and assess fully:

What is your face shape?
This helps you to decide on your best shapes for hair and glasses.

Are your features soft or sharp?
This decision helps you to select your most flattering collars, necklines and ties.

Face Geometry

On the whole, men are better at assessing their face shape than women. To start with this is probably because men usually have less hair – too much hair tends to obscure many women's face outline. If you do have long hair, or a particularly long fringe, you will need to push it back to assess the shape of your face accurately. Secondly, if you wear glasses you will need to remove them, as their shape may influence your judgement. (If you are blind as a bat without your glasses, you may need a loved one to assess your face shape for you!) Thirdly, pay no attention to the shape of your nose, mouth, cheeks and so on. Sometimes a man with very soft, or even chubby, features will see his face as round because of the influence of his features, even though the face shape itself is a square or rectangle.

With your hair pushed back (and glasses removed if necessary), study your face outline in a mirror – closing one eye can help. If you are feeling creative and happen to be in the bathroom, you can even dip your forefinger on to wet soap and trace round the outline of your face on the mirror. (Remember to clean the mirror afterwards or I shall be receiving letters from irate partners who have to clean up afterwards!)

Keep as close to the mirror as possible, or the outline you draw will be far too small to view properly. Stand back and assess the result.

Answering the following questions may help in your final analysis:

- Are the length and width equal? ☐
  Or is your face longer than it is wide? ☐
- Does the outline curve gently all the way round? ☐
  Or are the sides, top and jawline straighter? ☐
- Do you have a wide forehead and narrow chin? ☐
  Or a narrow forehead and wider jawline? ☐

The answers to all these questions, plus your general impression from the view in the mirror, will help ascertain your face shape and consequently help you decide on your best hairstyle and glasses. Study the drawings opposite with their accompanying descriptions, to see which one is closest to yours.

Is There an Ideal Shape?

Dismiss all notions of the 'perfect' face shape. Women often wish they had the perfect oval face and men often think of a long, chiselled face with a strong, distinctive jawline as the masculine ideal. Often, a man with a round face may buy square glasses in an attempt to square-up his face, or choose extra-long, pointed collars in a vain attempt to stretch his face downwards. Your face shape is down to your genes – it is the result of inherited bone structure and (barring drastic amounts of plastic surgery) there is not much you can do about it. What is important is to make the most of who and what you are rather than trying to change yourself into someone else. Most attempts to change a face dramatically, with glasses, collars, ties and so on, fail dramatically.

Analyzing Your Face Shape

Curved Outlines

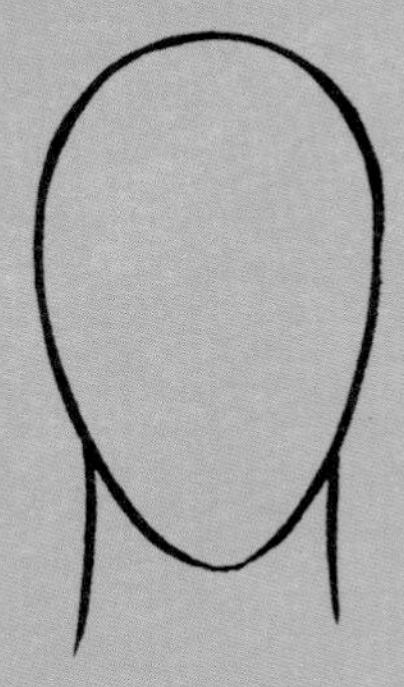

Oval
This face has gently curving sides and is longer than it is wide. The chin is slightly narrower than the forehead, resulting in an egg shape.

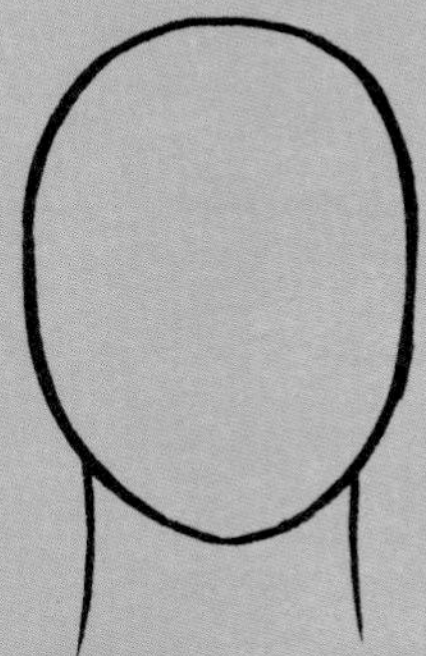

Round
This face has gently curving sides but its length and width are relatively equal, making it almost circular in shape.

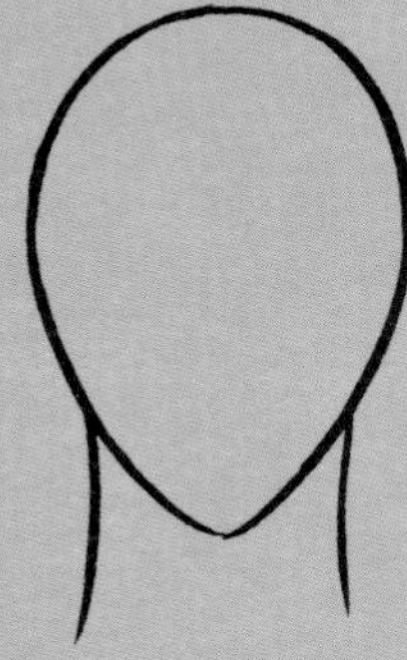

Heart
This face has a gently curving outline but the forehead is much wider than the chin, which can appear pointed.

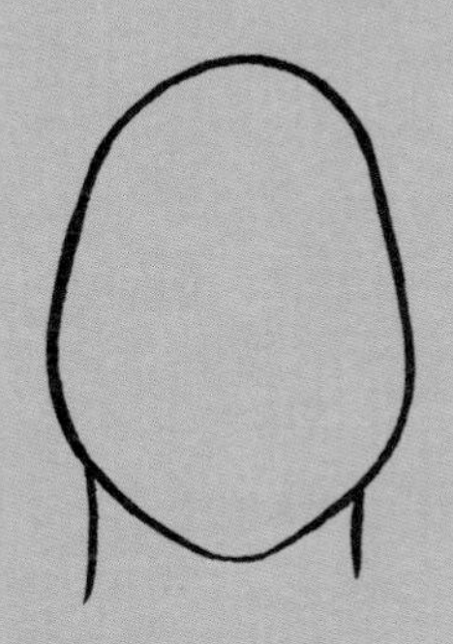

Pear
This face has gently curving sides but the jawline is wider than the forehead, giving quite an unusual face shape.

Angular Outlines

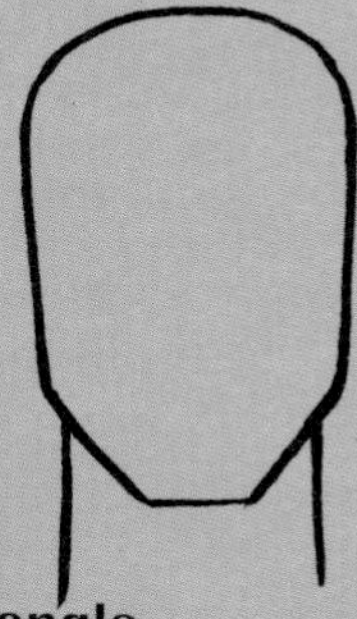

Rectangle
This face has straight sides and a square jaw, and the length is more than the width; it is often called an oblong face.

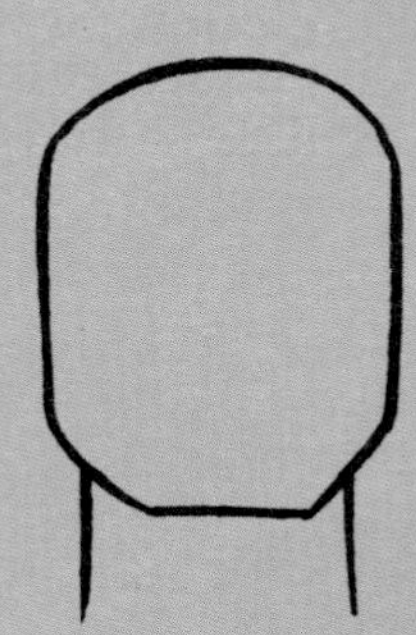

Square
This face has straight sides and a square jaw, but the length and width are relatively equal to produce quite a short face.

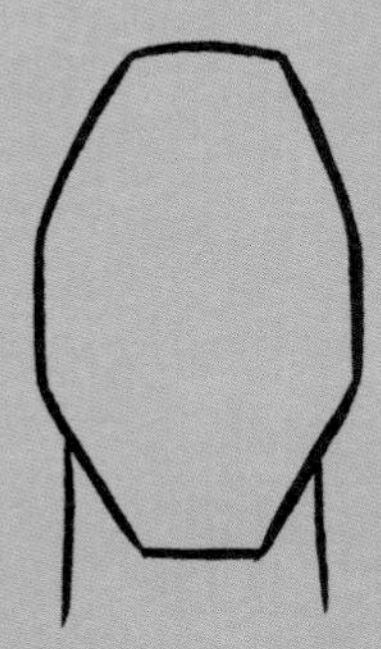

Diamond
This face has straight sides but a narrow forehead and chin – the cheekbones are the widest point.

You can make subtle changes to the apparent length and width of certain parts of your face by the way you choose the balance and proportion of your hair and glasses, but real, confident personal style is evident when you acknowledge and complement the real you.

Hair Today – Gone Tomorrow

All the suggestions below are, of course, based on the assumption that you have a full head of hair. If your rug is thinning, receding or has just plain disappeared for good, your option for creating balance and proportion with the best hairstyle are as reduced as the hairs on your head! In all these situations the advice is the same – accept who and what you are with confidence. In other words, don't try to pretend that you are not bald by combing a few strands across your head, or growing your hair extra long at the back to compensate for what is missing on the top. Such attempts to disguise or compensate simply

Hairstyles for Curved Outlines

Oval
An oval face can take most hairstyles because it is quite balanced, without any really extreme proportions. If, however, your face is a very long oval, you might benefit from a slight fringe to reduce its length slightly.

Round
As a round face is quite short, a heavy fringe can look disastrous. A clear forehead always looks best, or perhaps just a few wisps of fringe coming forward. A bit of height always benefits this face shape, so a layered cut, dried back with a mousse or gel (see Chapter 6), is advisable. Avoid fullness at the sides of the head – keep the cut very close around the ears with all the fullness on top.

Heart
This is a face shape which actually looks good with slightly longer hair. Because of the narrow chin, a hairstyle which has fullness around the neck looks balanced and well proportioned. Avoid a heavy fringe or a style which is very heavy on top as this will accentuate the narrow chin. An off-centre parting also looks good.

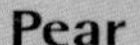

Pear
As this face is the opposite of the heart shape, the opposite advice is best. A style which is full and heavy on top acts as a good balance to the wide jawline. A hairstyle which is full around the neck area should be avoided – it is best to keep the neck area as shaven as possible.

draw attention to the situation. If your hair is receding or thinning on top it is always best to keep it short – the shorter the better. Most women will tell you that bold bald men, regardless of their face shape, can be extremely sexy; but insecure bald men with straggly, wispy long hairs can be a complete turn-off.

Long Hair

The majority of men prefer short hairstyles either because they work in a 'conventional' industry where it would look out of place to have long hair, or because they are not willing to put in the time and effort that long hair requires to keep it looking

Hairstyles for Angular Outlines

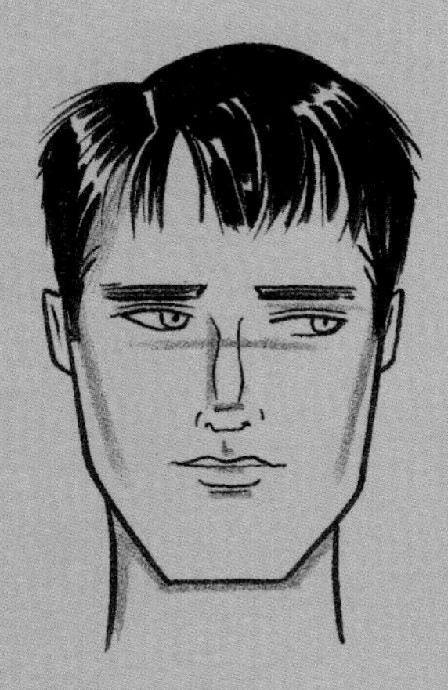

Rectangle
As this is a long face, a fringe, either full or partial, will always look good. Too much height on top should be avoided or the face will be extended even further and look out of proportion. Also, too much hair at the neckline should be avoided because of the wide jawline.

Square
Like a round face, this shape is very short, so a heavy fringe will simply reduce the face to an extremely small area which is not flattering. Height is needed, so short layers dried back with mousse or gel (see Chapter 6) are recommended. Fullness at the sides should be avoided, as this will make the face wider. Longer hair at the neckline and an off-centre parting can lengthen the face slightly.

Diamond
As this face has a narrow forehead and chin, it can take fullness in either or both of these areas. Fullness at the temples and in the neck area will both look good, but the hair should be cut close at the sides around the ears where the face is at its widest.

Above and right: A change of hairstyle, simply by using styling products, can be a quick and easy way to change your image from day to evening.

good. If you do work in a conventional office but want to hang on to the long hair of your youth, it is best to wear it tied back in a ponytail – especially if you have to wear a conventional suit and tie. Long hair is, however, very acceptable and even desirable in some industries such as advertising, music, media, fashion, theatre, and marketing. Today even sportsmen such as David Ginola and David Beckham have flowing locks, and sign lucrative advertising deals to use and promote certain haircare products. In fact, the secret of looking good with long hair lies in using the correct products and grooming techniques for your hair type (see Chapter 6 for full details).

Hair Makeover

If long hair is not cut regularly or looked after with the right products it will inevitably develop split ends and generally look unkempt and in poor condition. Mark (right) had not been to a hairdresser for several years having simply left his hair to grow below shoulder length. As well as split ends, he had the extra problem of dry ends with an oily scalp.

In this situation, the best solution is to cut off a substantial amount – not necessarily ultra-short but definitely above shoulder level to remove the most badly damaged section of hair. Our hairdresser, Paul Falltrick, cleansed and conditioned the hair with a dual action shampoo and conditioner and then combed the hair through with a wide-toothed comb which is always recommended for long hair.

Mark's hair was cut to just below the ears in a blunt shape to give it more volume and texture. The finished cut, which parts naturally at the centre, is worn behind the ears with just a sparing amount of gloss crème for a healthy shine. Still a casual, look, but a more groomed, dynamic image.

Specs Appeal – Have You Got It?

And so we move on from sex appeal in hairstyles to specs appeal in glasses. You might not have total control over the type of hair you have (or have not, as the case may be) but in the area of glasses you do have total control in the choices you make. Even if you don't wear prescription glasses (yet!) most men own sunglasses, and it is amazing what effect little pieces of plastic, metal and glass sitting on your nose can have on your image.

Glasses were once either an embarrassing sign of old age (the first step before the bus-pass and prostate problems) or the symbol of the school swot or nerd. Children were extremely cruel to their peers who wore glasses (especially the National Health Service variety), and many grown men today who wore glasses as children may have been deeply affected by such cruel taunts – an example of how appearance can affect our confidence even at a very young age.

Thankfully, over the past decade there has been a huge shift in attitude towards wearing glasses. Thanks to designers such as Armani and Gucci and celebrities like Chris Evans and Ronan Keating of Boyzone, who have all made glasses a fashionable and sexy accessory, children of the new millennium can now wear glasses with pride and panache! Many people now own several pairs to suit the different aspects of their lifestyle – a style for work, a style for sport and perhaps one that adjusts to light for summer. Most big-name designers are now producing seasonal ranges of eye-wear to complement their catwalk fashions, and glasses have become so much of a fashion accessory in London that they can be bought easily and cheaply with plain glass to enable those with good eyesight to look as young, hip and trendy as those who actually need them!

If you have to wear glasses all day long – or even for several hours of the day – they become a very important aspect of your appearance, and your choice of style, colour and fit is crucial to

Above: Eyewear for all occasions: serious frames for work; a lighter style for evening; and coloured lenses for fun.

everyone's perception of you. As with hairstyles, just bear your face shape in mind to find your best shape (see next page).

Size Matters

- For glasses to look balanced on your face, the top of the frame should follow your eyebrows as closely as possible – either directly on the eyebrow or below it. Glasses which extend above the eyebrow give a 'double-eyebrow' effect and a look of constant surprise.
- The sides of the frame should not extend greatly beyond the sides of your face. Frames which extend too far beyond the sides of the head give the wearer an uncanny resemblance to Brains, the *Thunderbirds* puppet!
- The bottom of the frame should definitely not be touching your cheeks – the most common mistake! Glasses which rest too low on the cheek leave the eye 'floating' at the top of the lens like a goldfish surfacing in its bowl – your eye should be in the centre of the lens.

Weighty Problems

If you are short or have light bone structure, it is easy to look overwhelmed in heavy glasses; a small frame in a lightweight metal, or even a frameless style is more flattering. If you are of a big build or have heavier bone structure, very small, delicate glasses would look out of place. Opt instead for larger frames in a heavy acetate which would be more complementary to your scale.

Instant Nose Job

A long, thin nose can be shortened by the right glasses – choose ones with a low bridge for a nose job without surgery! Conversely, if you have the flat, 'squashed' variety of nose, a very high bridge will create the illusion of a longer, slimmer nose.

Seeing Eye to Eye

Wide-set eyes can be brought closer together with a dark, heavy bridge, while close-set eyes will have more space created between them with a clear, transparent bridge.

Glasses for Curved Outlines

Oval

Most shapes of frames will suit you, so to narrow down your choice and make a definite statement, use the softness or angularity of your features to help you make your selection (see later in this chapter). Oval faces can often look good in frames slightly wider than the face, especially if the face is a long oval.

Round

Avoid round glasses, which will echo and emphasize your face shape. Gentle ovals or softened squares are most flattering. A clear bridge will help to narrow your face, and high-set arms will add extra length.

Heart-Shaped

Avoid shapes with a heavy top frame such as aviator styles, as these will emphasize the width of your forehead. Fullness at the bottom of the glasses or low-set arms are flattering to balance your narrow chin area. Sharp or softened rectangles also look good.

Pear-Shaped

A wide or heavy top to the frame is good to broaden the forehead and balance the chin. Avoid fullness at the bottom of the glasses and low-set arms, which draw attention to the chin. Styles which are frameless at the bottom are also a good choice.

Creative or Classic?

The advice I have given on glasses assumes, of course, that you would like the frames to complement your face. This is true of the majority of people. Some men, however – especially extrovert, creative types or showbiz personalities – deliberately break the rules to make their glasses a dominant feature of their appearance. Small, round glasses on a large, round face (Lenny Henry) or large square glasses on a small square face (Chris Evans) are 'wrong' in shape, weight and scale, and result in an almost comic look which needs a great deal of confidence and personality to carry off well. A similar effect can be achieved by selecting a colour of frame which clashes with your own colouring (see Chapter 4 for recommended colours of frames).

Glasses for Angular Outlines

Rectangle

As this face is longer than it is wide, frames which shorten or widen the face are best. Deep or square glasses work well. Low-set arms or a low bridge will also help shorten the face. If you are already shortening your face with a fringe, wide rectangles can be very flattering. If you have no fringe, however, a heavy horizontal line across the top of the glasses has a similar effect.

Square

This face needs to be lengthened, so frames which are quite shallow – ovals or rectangles – work best. High-set arms will also lengthen the face, and a clear bridge will help narrow it slightly. Heavy or contrasting vertical sides to the frames will add to the illusion of extra length – avoid very square glasses at all costs.

Diamond

Frames that will add width to the forehead and/or chin work best. If you are widening your forehead with a fringe, you may want to have glasses with fullness just at the bottom. If you are widening your chin with a longish hairstyle, frames with width at the top only may be best. If you want to widen your forehead and chin, aviator-style glasses are ideal. Avoid styles which are wide at the cheekbones or have thick, heavy arms.

Facial Features and Their Effects

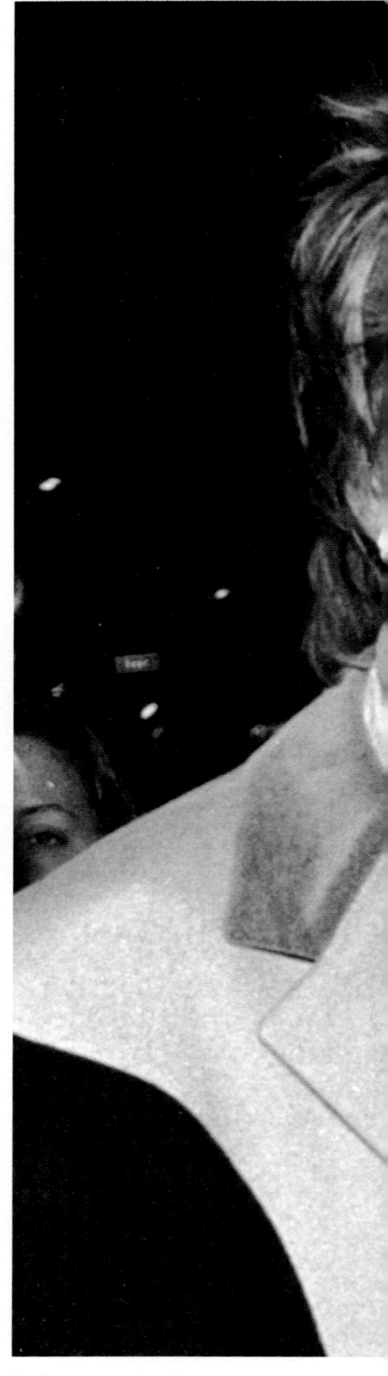

Soft or angular features can be equally attractive if like Leonardo Di Caprio (left) and Rod Stewart (right), you confidently emphasize them with your hairstyle.

So far I have dealt only with the top half of your face. We now need to look at collars, ties and necklines to complete the picture. If your features are mostly soft (Leonardo Di Caprio) you will be well suited to contoured patterns on ties and should choose collars and necklines which are not too severe. If your features are mostly sharp (Rod Stewart) you will be best suited to strong patterns near the face and to necklines which are quite sharp and angular. As with glasses and hairstyles, it is best to go with what you are rather than fight against it or try to change yourself.

Look at the descriptions opposite and tick the boxes which most accurately describe your features. If you find this difficult because you are too familiar with your own face, you may want to ask that loved one again to help you in your decisions!

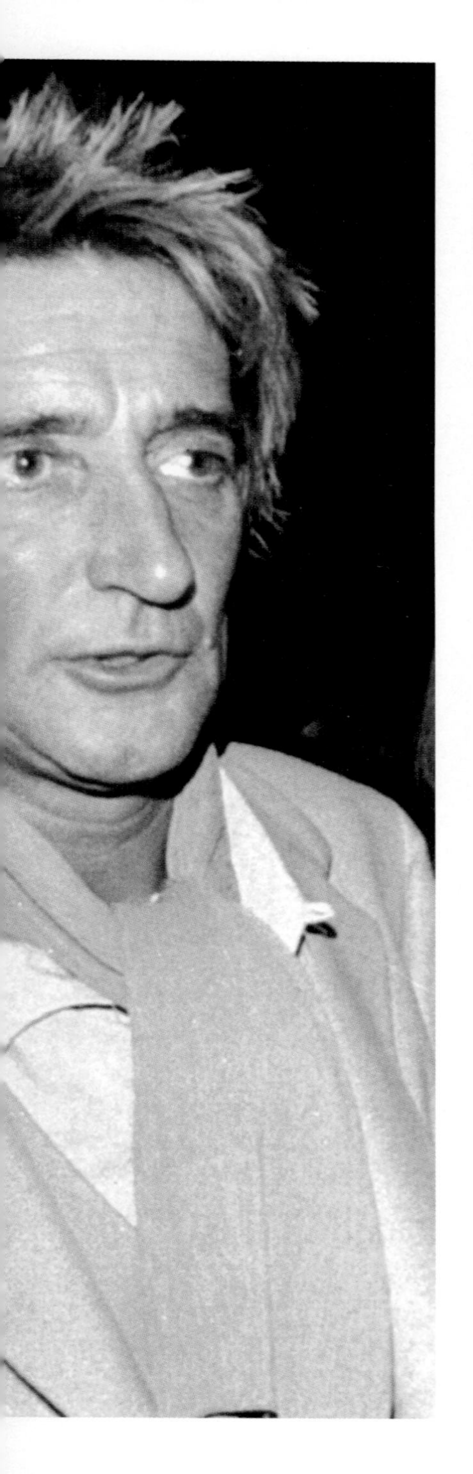

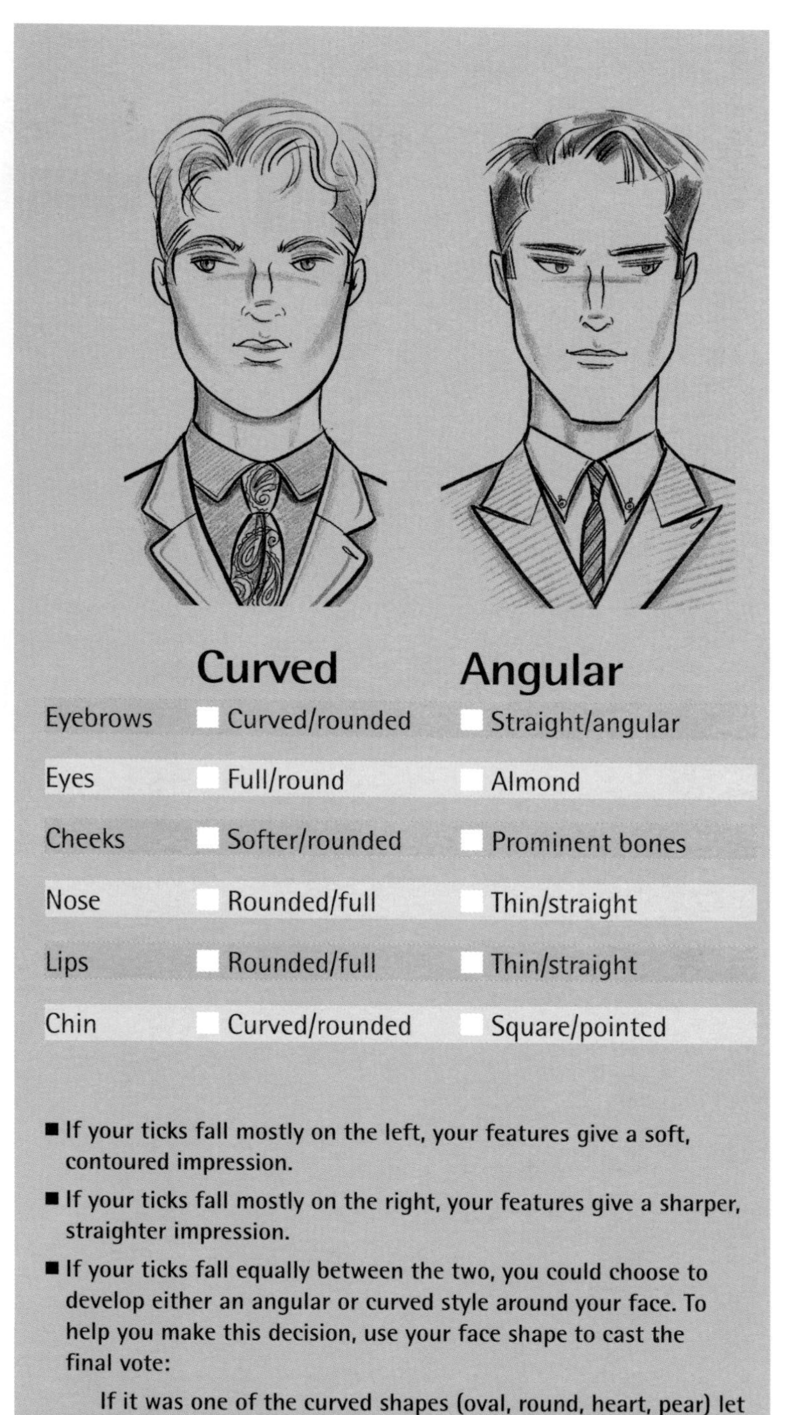

	Curved	Angular
Eyebrows	☐ Curved/rounded	☐ Straight/angular
Eyes	☐ Full/round	☐ Almond
Cheeks	☐ Softer/rounded	☐ Prominent bones
Nose	☐ Rounded/full	☐ Thin/straight
Lips	☐ Rounded/full	☐ Thin/straight
Chin	☐ Curved/rounded	☐ Square/pointed

- If your ticks fall mostly on the left, your features give a soft, contoured impression.
- If your ticks fall mostly on the right, your features give a sharper, straighter impression.
- If your ticks fall equally between the two, you could choose to develop either an angular or curved style around your face. To help you make this decision, use your face shape to cast the final vote:

  If it was one of the curved shapes (oval, round, heart, pear) let that be the chosen direction for your style; if it was one of the angular shapes (rectangle, square, diamond) let that be the chosen direction for your style. It is always best to develop a consistent, definite look around your face so that your glasses, collars, ties and so on all work together in a stylish way.

Curved Features

If you have curved features the following details beneath the face will be most flatttering.

Collars
Standard collar
Spread collar
Rounded collar
Button-down in soft fabric

Spread collar

Patterns
(Ties and shirts)
Plain fabric
Blended stripes
Soft checks
Swirls, flowers, paisley, polka-dots

Standard collar

Lapels
Notched
Rounded
Nehru

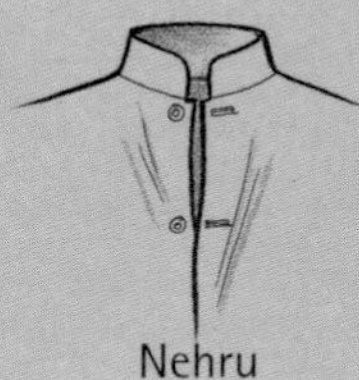

Nehru

Necklines
Crew-neck
Bagel-neck
'Granddad'-collar
Drawstring neckline

Notched lapel

Bagel-neck

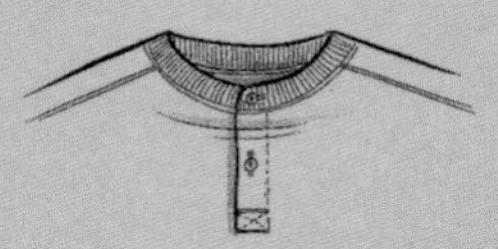

'Granddad'-collar

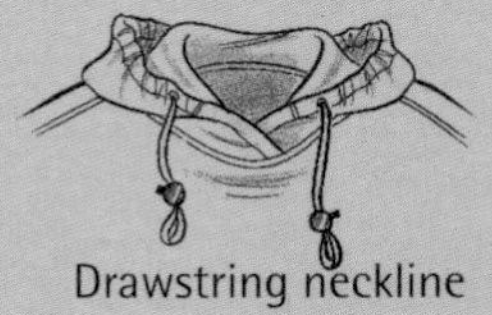

Drawstring neckline

Angular Features

If you have angular features the following details beneath the face will be most flatttering

Collars
- Standard collar
- Pin collar
- Tab collar
- Button-down in crisp fabric

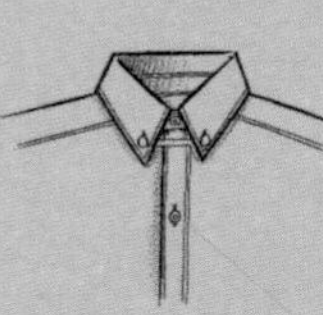
Tab collar

Patterns
- Plain fabric
- Sharp stripes
- Bold checks
- Geometrics, zig-zags, diamonds, pin dots

Button-down

Lapels
- Notched
- Peaked
- Mandarin

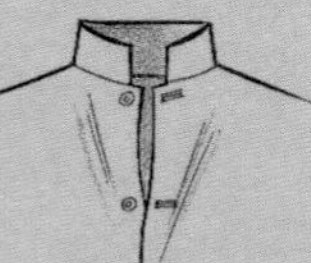
Mandarin

Necklines
- V-neck
- Turtle-neck
- Polo-shirt
- Zip-up neckline

Peaked lapel

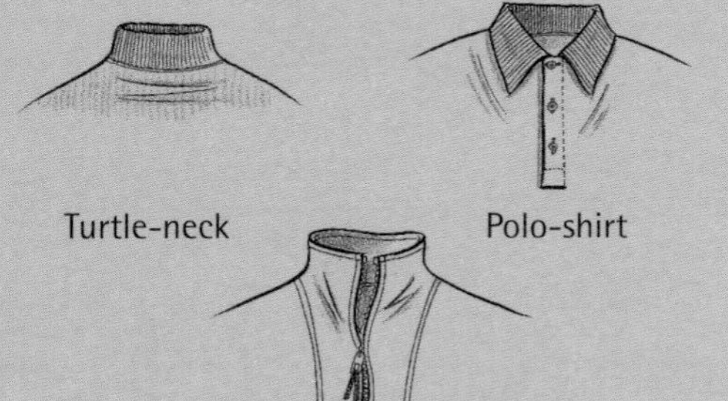
Turtle-neck
Polo-shirt

Zip-up neckline

Far Left: Soft faces are best complemented by ties with curved or contoured patterns.
Left: Angular faces are best complemented by ties with sharp or geometric patterns.

Knotty Problems

The width of your tie-knot should always complement your choice of collar. If you have a soft face, a standard spread or rounded collar will always look better with a double Windsor knot. If you have an angular face, a standard, pin, tab or button-down collar will suit you best with a thinner four in hand knot.

Four in Hand Knot

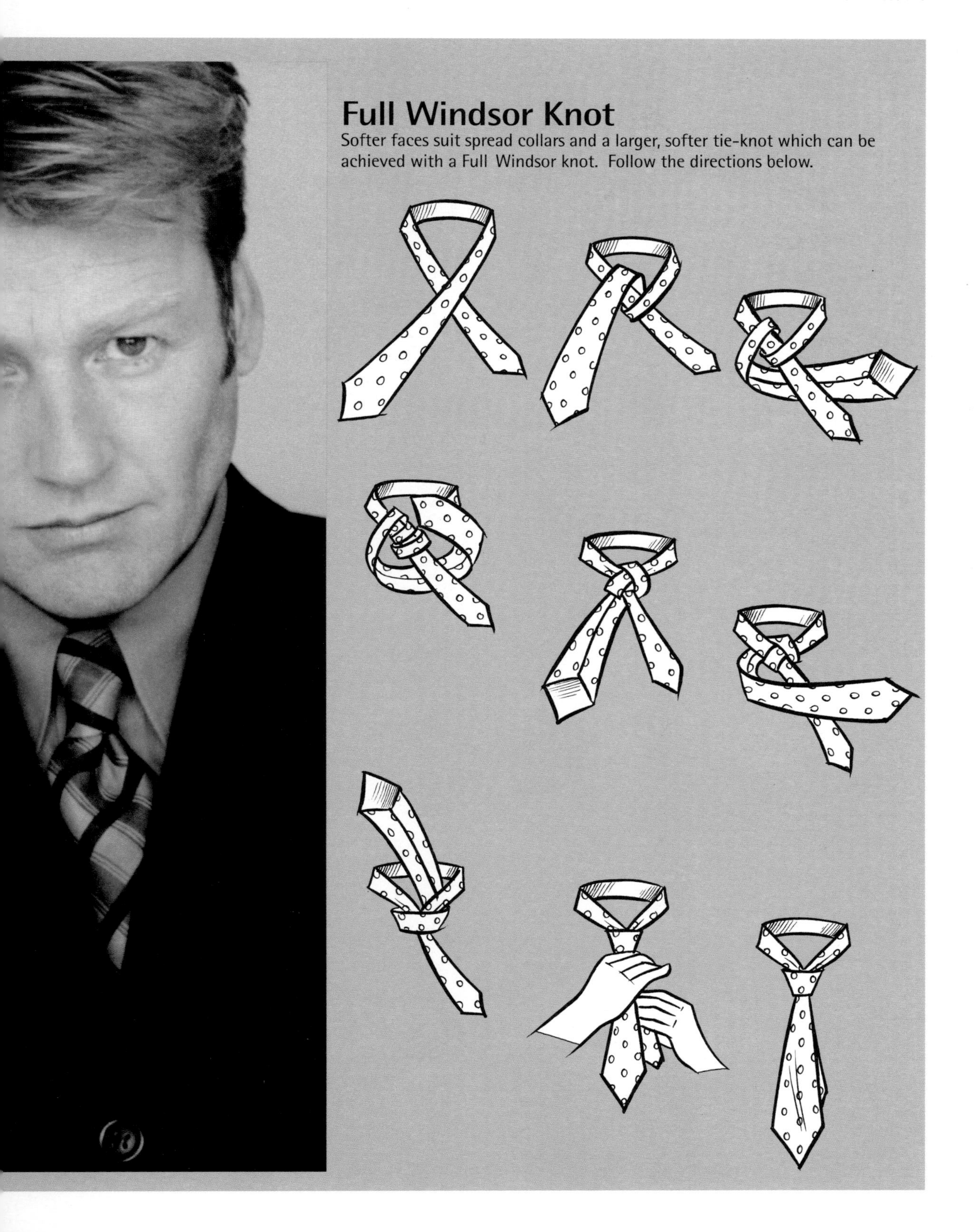

Full Windsor Knot

Softer faces suit spread collars and a larger, softer tie-knot which can be achieved with a Full Windsor knot. Follow the directions below.

Chapter 3

Body Directions

Suits You, Sir!

Above: Understanding your Body Direction is the key to finding your most flattering garments from workwear to beachwear.

For your clothes to look good on you, and for you to feel comfortable and confident in them, they need to fit perfectly and look as though they were made for you. Men who can afford the luxury of a made-to-measure suit will know what a difference it makes to wear clothes which feel like a natural extension of the body – almost like a second skin which fits and hangs perfectly rather than pulling or sagging in various places.

But few men can afford the expensive expertise of experienced tailors, and few men today spend the majority of their time in a formal suit anyway. In fact, as our society becomes increasingly less formal and more relaxed, only one in three men are now wearing a traditional suit, shirt and tie in their working environment. So, although it is important to know which cut of suit is best for you for occasions which demand it, it is just as important to understand how to select your best styles for casual and semi-casual wear.

Wearing a suit was always a relatively safe option for most men who wanted to look their best. Looking good in today's more relaxed, casual environment presents men with far more clothing dilemmas and far more opportunities to go hopelessly wrong in their choice. Men have now entered that dangerous zone that women have found themselves in for decades, where there is so much choice and flexibility that looking good on a day-to-day basis becomes very much a hit and miss affair.

Your Body Blueprint

What you need is a full understanding of your body – its bone structure and the way your flesh and muscle are arranged around it. Your basic body shape is genetically predetermined, but you can work out to build up muscle in certain areas and reduce fat in others to change your natural shape to one you consider more attractive. There will always be certain aspects of your physique over which you have no control because they are determined by bone structure – for example, length of neck, arms, legs and width and shape of your ribcage.

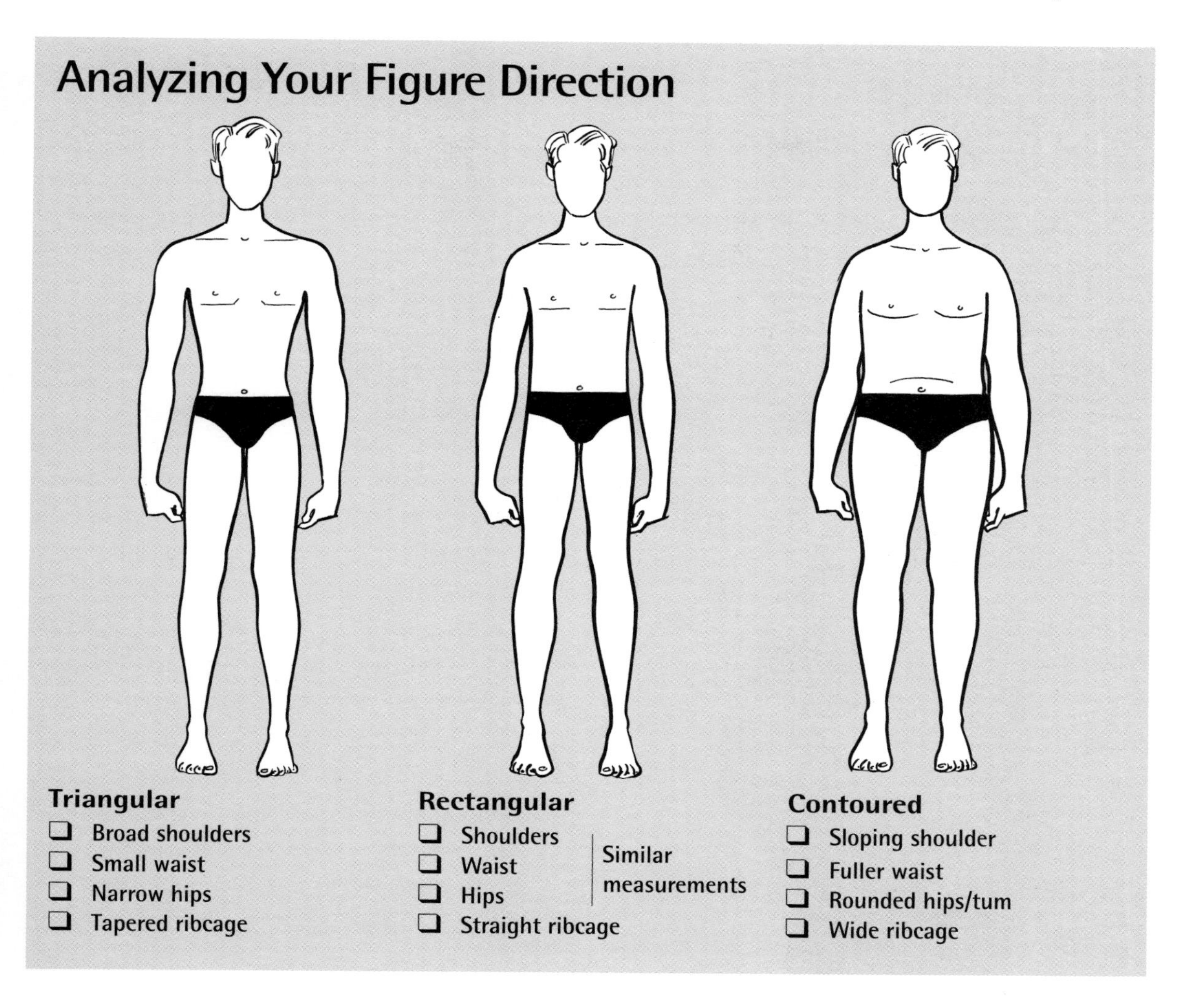

To gain complete knowledge of your body's blueprint you first need to understand the shape of your exterior silhouette and which styles of clothing are most flattering to it. Secondly, you need to assess all the different proportions of your body (your good parts and your not-so-good ones!) and learn how to adapt your best basic styles to achieve your ultimate look for all occasions – smart, casual and semi-casual. Let's look first at your body's outline or exterior silhouette, which from now on I will call your Body Direction.

Either picture yourself in your underwear or stand in front of a full length mirror with next to nothing on and compare your body with the drawings above. Tick the boxes for the silhouette which most closely resembles your own.

Defining Your Body Direction

You will probably find it easier to define your Body Direction than you did to define your Face Direction – also, you'll be pleased to know that you don't have to make a mess of the bathroom mirror! On the whole I find that men are very honest about their bodies, while women often have a very distorted view of what shape they actually are.

Triangular Body Direction

This body has a shoulder measurement which is much bigger than the waist and hip measurements, giving the overall look of an inverted triangle. Some men naturally have this body shape, whilst others work out to build up the muscles in the upper chest and the shoulders to achieve this look. Sometimes a man whose job involves a lot of physical work and heavy lifting will achieve this shape by accident. You do not, however, have to be big, tall and muscle-bound to be this shape – you may, indeed, look like Arnold Shwarzenegger but you may also be shorter or slighter, like Sebastian Coe, and still have a triangular silhouette. Remember that the defining feature of this shape is the fact that the shoulders are much wider than the waist and hips, resulting in a tapered look to the ribcage.

Left: The Triangular Body Direction has a wide chest and shoulders in comparison to a small waist, hips and bottom.
Top right: The Rectangular Body Direction has shoulders, chest, waist and hips all with similar measurements.
Right: The Contoured Body Direction has a softer shoulder line, a wider waistline and rounded hips and bottom.

Rectangular Body Direction

The majority of men have this straight body outline, with shoulders, ribcage, waist and hips being of roughly equal measurements, resulting in a rectangular shape. You may be quite slim (like Tony Blair) or more stout (like Bill Clinton), but if your shoulders, ribs, waist and hips have similar measurements your body is definitely rectangular. Many men with this physique often wish that they were more triangular, as they perceive that shape as more masculine and therefore more attractive to women! Research has shown, however, that most women find the rectangular body shape just as attractive as the triangular one so long as the man is fit, healthy and not too thin. An excessively muscular triangular shape achieved by working out can, in fact, be less attractive than this more streamlined silhouette. A man with this latter body shape has the most options when selecting clothing styles, because his body is not too extreme in any of its dimensions.

Contoured Body Direction

Although this body shape is still quite rectangular in shape, it has the appearance of much softer edges which are characterized by the more rounded look to the shoulder and hip line. This may be a man who once had a more rectangular or triangular shape but has put on a few extra pounds, or he may be a naturally large-boned man who is often described as 'stocky' or 'solid' in appearance. Like the other two silhouettes, this man may be short or tall, but normally such a physique will include a thickish neck and substantial arms and legs. Having a contoured shape does not necessarily mean overweight or unfit – it simply means a more rounded look to the body. Frank Bruno, Phil Collins and William Hague all have a contoured look and are ideal weights for their height and bone structure. Choosing the best garments for this bodyshape is extremely important in order to achieve an attractive, comfortable and confident look.

Shop for the Real You

Having established whether you have a Triangular, Rectangular or more Contoured Body Direction, we can now look at your best basic style of clothing to make the most of your shape and develop your very best personal style. It is important to keep your own blueprint in mind when shopping and not be tempted to buy an item because you have seen it look good on someone else or simply because it is in fashion at the moment. A double-breasted blazer may look good on a slim, Triangular man like Sebastian Coe but would be a disaster on a short, Contoured man like Danny De Vito!

What every man has to realize is that the reason something looks good on someone else is, very often, because that person is inside it. When you put something similar on your completely different shape, the result may be an eyesore or, worse still, comical! In the male fashion world today there is something to suit every man, no matter what his shape or size. All it needs is careful selection from the stores or mail-order services to select your most flattering garments year after year. With formal suits, shirts and ties disappearing in the corporate world it is important for businessmen in particular to choose less formal garments carefully in order to retain a professional and credible look.

Below: It is important for businessmen in particular to chose their garments carefully in order to retain a professional and credible look.

Garments to Suit your Body Direction

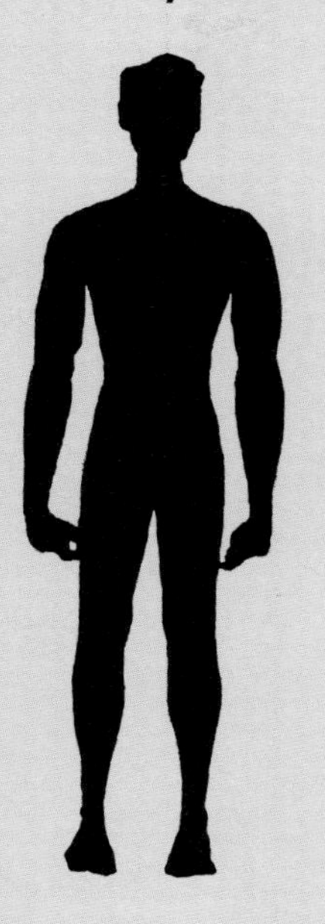

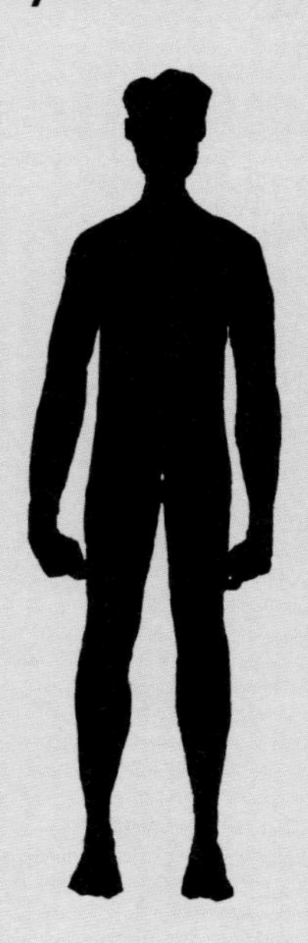

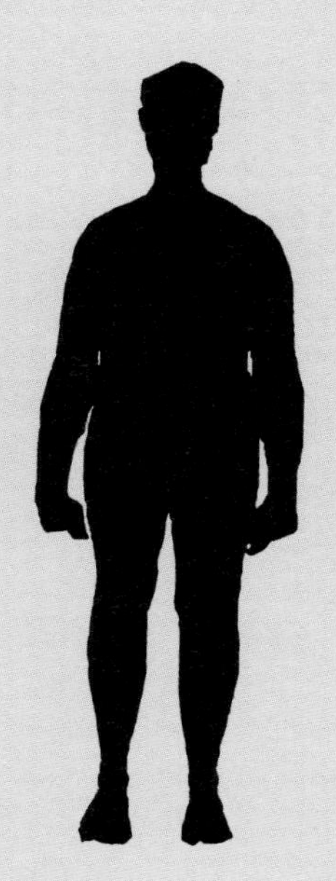

	Triangular	Rectangular	Contoured
Formal jackets	Little or no padding Wide/peaked lapels Double-breasted Angular hemline	Substantial padding Notched/peaked lapels Double/single-breasted Angular/curved hemline	Moderate padding Rounded/notched lapels Single-breasted Curved hemline
Casual jackets/ coats	Jeans jackets Bomber jackets Blouson jackets Belted trench coat	Zip-front jackets Reefer jackets Crombie overcoat Back-belted trench coat	Melton jackets (felty fabric) Long-line jackets Duffel coat Straight raincoat
Formal/ casual trousers	Double pleats Slim-fit Tapered leg Belt on show	Single pleats Regular-fit Straight leg Belt shown or covered	Flat-fronted Relaxed-fit Straight leg Belt covered
Casual tops	Tucked in Slim-fitting Short lengths	Worn in or out Straight shapes Moderate lengths	Worn outside Vertical designs Longer length
Swimwear/ shorts	Slim-fit trunks Football shorts Belted waistline	Shorts-style trunks Chino shorts Belted or not	Long-length trunks Drawstring shorts Not belted

Guidelines for Triangular Body Direction

Although you have a good selection of clothes to choose from, avoid exaggerating your shoulders too much (such as excessive padding in jackets) or your body may tend to look out of proportion. Because of your wide shoulders you can, however, take quite wide lapels (even exaggerated peaks if your face is angular too), and double-breasted jackets will always look good. Your narrow waist and hips mean that casual jackets that end at the waistline, or longer jackets with a tight drawstring waist, will be flattering. Long, unstructured jackets, casual shirts worn outside your trousers and loose, baggy sweaters which fall directly down from your wide shoulders can be unflattering, as they will hide your slim waist and hips and make you appear wider or fatter than you actually are. Tops tucked in look best (even sweaters, if you are very slim), and you will always suit having a belt on show. This figure looks great without a jacket and will find most types of swimwear easy to wear – even the very tight styles! Because of your slim hips, trousers with double pleats or tight, figure-hugging jeans both look good. Tightly woven fabrics and shiny finishes to garments will also complement your sharp, angular look more than loose weaves or soft, nubby textures.

A. Double-breasted suit with peaked lapels, double vents, square hemline, flap pockets and double-pleated trousers worn with formal button-down shirt and diagonal-stripe tie.

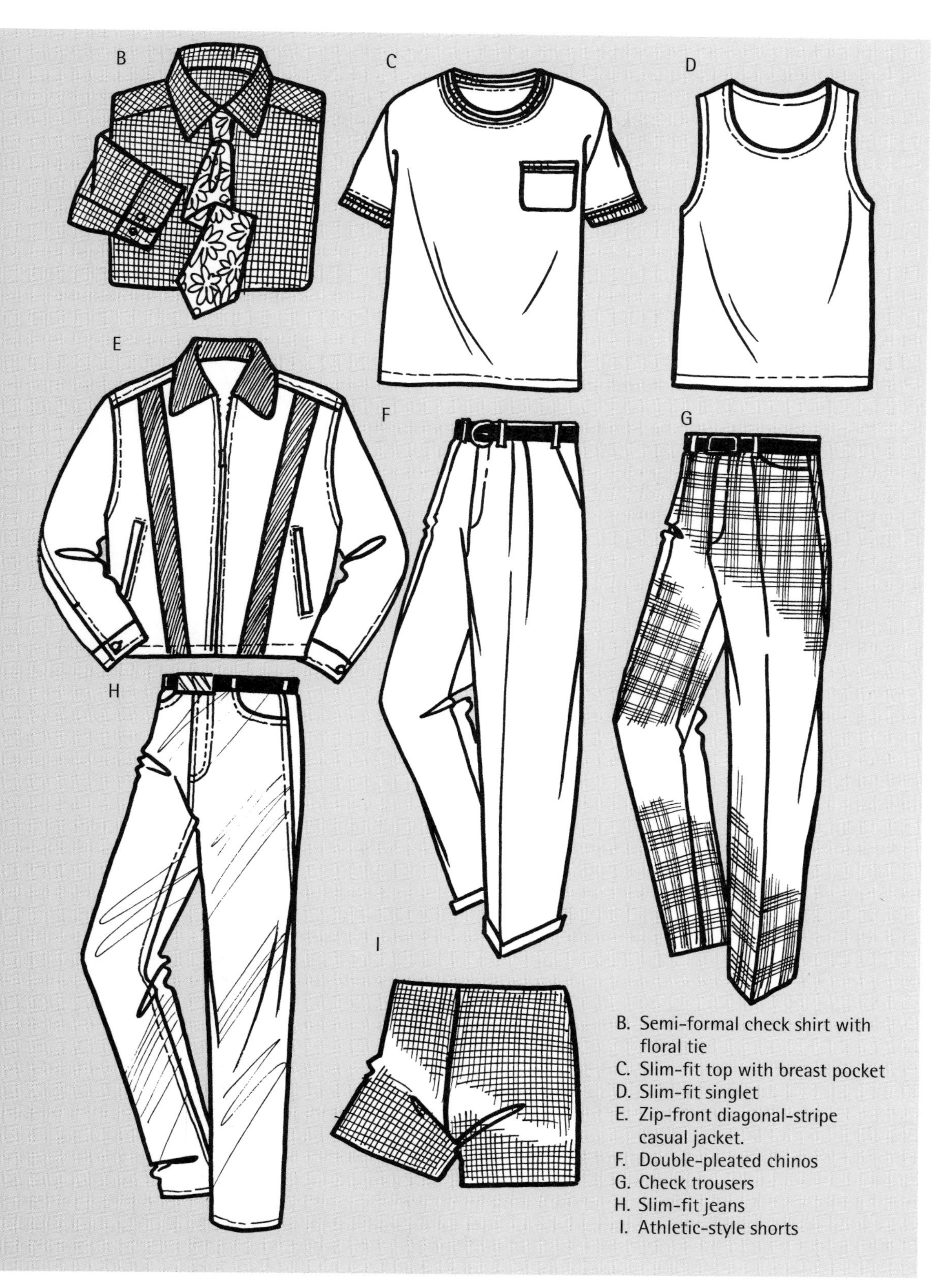

B. Semi-formal check shirt with floral tie
C. Slim-fit top with breast pocket
D. Slim-fit singlet
E. Zip-front diagonal-stripe casual jacket.
F. Double-pleated chinos
G. Check trousers
H. Slim-fit jeans
I. Athletic-style shorts

Guidelines for Rectangular Body Direction

To give yourself a rather more dynamic look you can select clothing which gives the illusion of a slightly wider top half, for instance jackets with shoulder padding, sweaters with chest stripes, and slightly peaked lapels. If you are slim, double-breasted jackets with two vents will look good but if you are more portly, single-breasted jackets with only one vent will be more flattering. The best casual jackets for you are straight-cut and slightly longer than waist-length – zip-front cagoules and reefer jackets look good. Casual shirts or T-shirts can be either tucked in or left outside your trousers or shorts, as this will not have any effect on your perceived shape – do whatever is most comfortable or right for the image you wish to project.

Like the Triangular man, you can look good without a jacket; but you may find very tight swimming trunks unflattering without the broad shoulders they require – shorts-style swimwear will be more flattering. Again, avoid very figure-hugging jeans as these also require broad shoulders to look their best – double- or single-pleated chinos will be your most flattering casual trousers. Being the man-in-the-middle, who is neither very angular nor very contoured in shape, you can choose from a greater range of fabrics – from tightly woven, crisp materials to more loosely woven, softer textures, depending on your preference.

A. Single-breasted suit with notched lapels, single-vent, square hemline, flap pockets and single-pleated trousers worn with formal standard-collar shirt and horizontal-stripe tie.

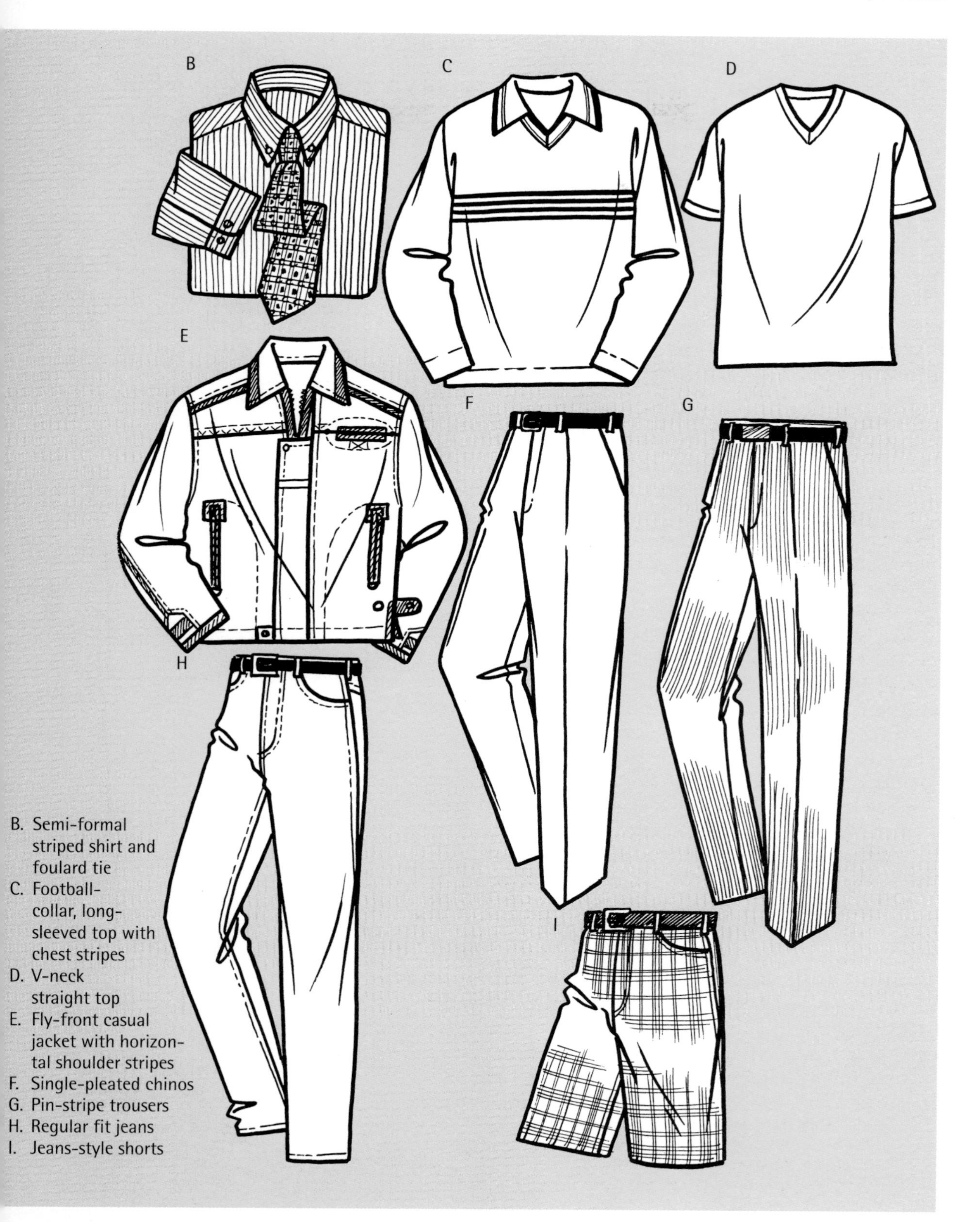

B. Semi-formal striped shirt and foulard tie
C. Football-collar, long-sleeved top with chest stripes
D. V-neck straight top
E. Fly-front casual jacket with horizontal shoulder stripes
F. Single-pleated chinos
G. Pin-stripe trousers
H. Regular fit jeans
I. Jeans-style shorts

Guidelines for Contoured Body Direction

Since you have more rounded lines to your silhouette, it is best to avoid any clothing that has a very sharp, angular look as this will conflict with your shape and be most unflattering – a double-breasted, pin-striped suit with big peaked lapels and huge trouser turn-ups on a man with this body shape always gives a 'gangster' look! As well as looking more stylish, you will be far more comfortable in an easy, unconstructed suit with moderate lapels, no vents at the back and definitely a single-breasted closure. Crisply tailored double-breasted jackets are your worst look – especially when the jacket is left open, as the double amount of fabric at the front will make you look doubly wide.

Casual jackets should also be roomy and at least knuckle-length, with no waist emphasis – leave drawstring waists on parkas untied. Your casual shirts, T-shirts and sweaters need to stress the vertical in their design – go for ribs, cables, seams or stripes running up and down the garment – and will always look best worn outside your trousers or shorts. When wearing a formal shirt and tie, it is more difficult for you to go without a jacket and still look smart and authoritative because of your 'softer' look. For this reason, waistcoats are an excellent addition for a more contoured man when buying a suit. They will allow him to go jacket-less in summer months while retaining a lengthening look and some degree of sharpness to his body.

Also, don't make the mistake of thinking that a figure with bigger hips/tum needs double-pleated trousers – flat-fronted (in other words darted rather than pleated) trousers are actually your most flattering design for either formal or casual trousers. Swimwear and shorts will look best in longer lengths (again stressing the vertical) with adjustable drawstring waists. Finally, your best fabrics will be soft and loosely woven – avoid anything which is too tightly woven, sharp, crisp or shiny.

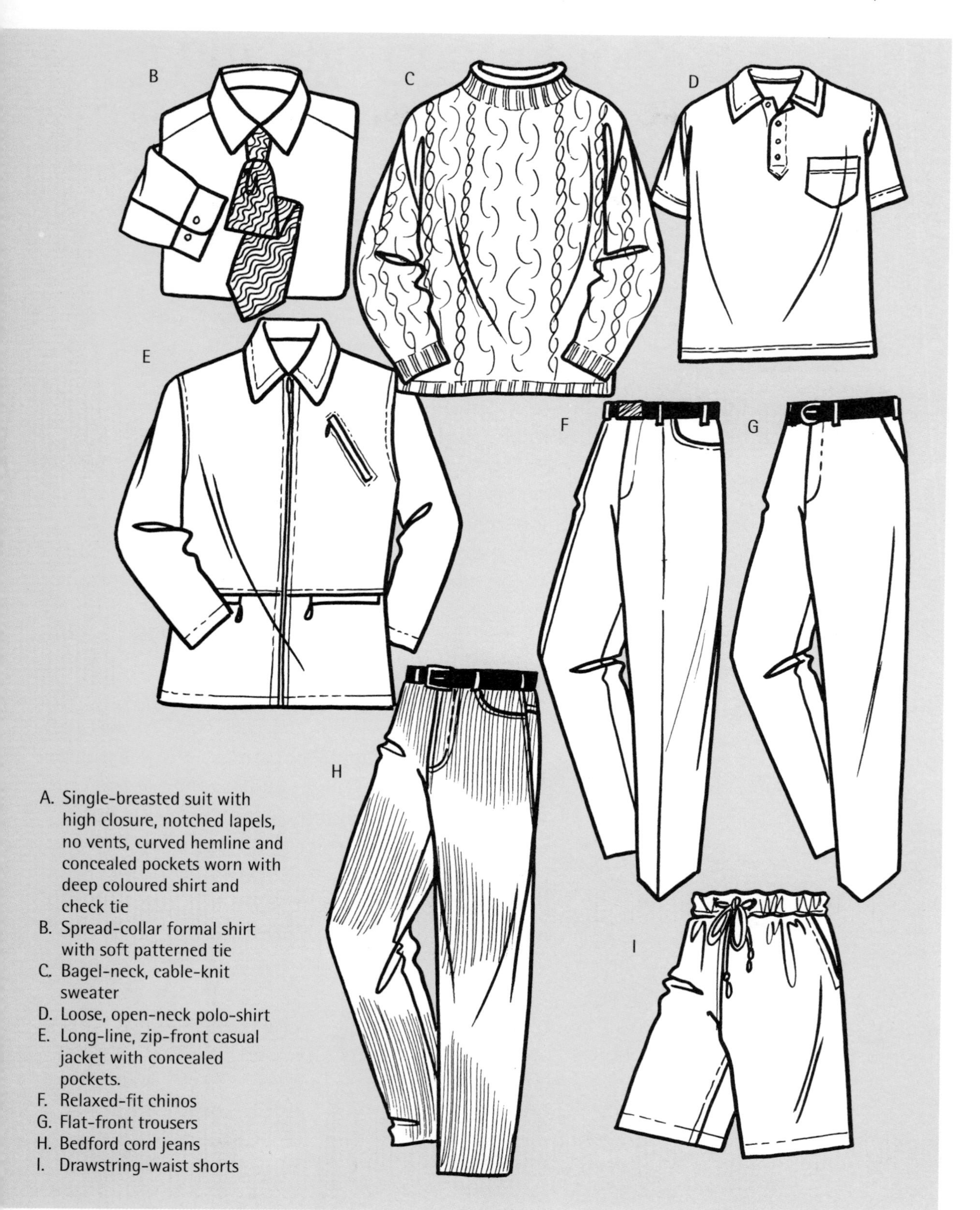

A. Single-breasted suit with high closure, notched lapels, no vents, curved hemline and concealed pockets worn with deep coloured shirt and check tie
B. Spread-collar formal shirt with soft patterned tie
C. Bagel-neck, cable-knit sweater
D. Loose, open-neck polo-shirt
E. Long-line, zip-front casual jacket with concealed pockets.
F. Relaxed-fit chinos
G. Flat-front trousers
H. Bedford cord jeans
I. Drawstring-waist shorts

Your Proportions and How to Manipulate Them

Below: A horizontal stripe can make a narrow chest look wider.

Right: Pinstripes will make you look taller and slimmer.

Now that you have worked out the most important aspect of your body, your Body Direction, all you need to know are the little tricks of the trade to draw the viewer's eye away from your not-so-good points. Let's not stop at that, though, because the following information will also help you to draw attention to the best bits of your body if you want to – rather than dwelling on the negatives, think how you can use this advice to make the most of your assets!

To understand how to manipulate the viewer's idea of your shape or create illusions about certain areas of your body, you need a basic understanding of how line, fabric, colour and scale can affect our perception of objects, including bodies. The most important of these four is line – horizontals, verticals and diagonals, believe it or not, all play a big part in your appearance.

Line

Horizontal lines

Research has shown that the eye travels down an object from top to bottom. If there are no horizontal lines across the object it normally travels quite quickly down the object and then up to the top again. However, whenever the eye comes to a horizontal line it is arrested at that point, scans across the line and then continues on its journey. Although you are not aware of it, this is what happens when you look at someone else and what happens when that person looks at you. Consequently, you never

want to put a horizontal line across a part of your body that you don't like or that you don't want to draw attention to.

Most people know that horizontal stripes on a sweatshirt are widening – rugby shirts have 'hoops' to make the players appear broader and bulkier. It is not just stripes, however, which we need to consider when thinking about horizontal lines. Pockets often have strong horizontal lines, which is why the big patch pockets on the back of jeans are a disaster on men with large bottoms! The hemlines of jackets, sweaters, T-shirts and so on will draw attention to that part of your body like a band going round a barrel, which is why they should not end around your bottom if it is on the large side. Some necklines also have a great horizontal hold on the eye – polo-necks and turtle-necks, for instance will both shorten and broaden your neck considerably. Knowing where and where not to put your horizontals is therefore vital.

Vertical lines

On the other hand, vertical lines are much more lengthening and slimming. They accelerate the eye on its journey up and down the body, almost like giving it train tracks to travel on. The result is that plenty of vertical lines in an outfit will make the wearer appear taller and slimmer; this is why footballers wear vertical stripes rather than horizontal, because speed and agility are meant to be their key qualities rather than bulk or brawn. If you are short and/or overweight, having vertical lines in your outfit (while eliminating as many horizontals as possible) is very important. Only the very tall and/or very underweight will want to avoid too many verticals in their outfits and stress the horizontal instead.

Again, don't think of verticals as just stripes on a fabric. Strong vertical lines can be created by obvious seams, cables, ribs, colour blocks and single-breasted buttons. Some trousers and jackets have vertical pockets set into side seams, which can be much more flattering than horizontal or patch pockets. An outfit with an abundance of vertical lines, such as a pin-stripe suit (single-breasted jacket and no turn-ups on the trousers) worn with a vertically striped tie and a straight, single-breasted coat, is one of the most slimming and lengthening looks that can be achieved by any man.

Above: A diagonal shoulder seam will reduce broad shoulders – men with narrow/sloping shoulders should avoid this style.

Diagonal lines

If horizontals arrest the eye and are widening, and verticals speed up the eye and are lengthening, diagonals come somewhere in between in their ability to have these effects on your body. Basically, the closer a diagonal line comes to a vertical, the more lengthening and slimming it is; the closer it comes to a horizontal, the more arresting and widening it is. You may think that diagonals don't occur very often in clothing, but again, if you think beyond the notion of a stripe in the fabric, diagonals are actually quite common.

A V-neck is made up of diagonals, and therefore the deeper it is the more lengthening it becomes to a thick neck. A raglan sleeve (see above) puts a diagonal line across the shoulders and is therefore good at diminishing too broad shoulders but disastrous for narrow or sloping ones. Pockets set at an angle on the back of jeans, or a dipped yoke at the back, can help reduce a large bottom.

Fabric

Choice of fabric also affects focal points on the body and the apparent size of various parts. As with horizontal lines, the eye is arrested by and zooms in on the light or bright aspects of an outfit. Because shiny fabrics reflect light and appear bright they draw attention to themselves. The reflection of the light also makes the part of the body they cover appear larger. A shiny nylon football shirt will therefore draw attention to a beer belly and make it appear larger, and shiny shell suits were the worst fashion ever foisted on overweight males. Tight, shiny swimming trunks will enlarge the bottoms they encase – the plus side is that they will also increase the apparent size of your front assets! (The ideal swimming trunks for most men would have a shiny front with horizontal lines and a dark back with vertical lines.)

By now you've probably worked out that matt fabrics have the opposite effect to shiny – they don't draw attention and can reduce the size of the parts they cover. Matt fabrics absorb the light and will therefore make the body appear firmer and slimmer. Returning to our examples above, a cotton football shirt and a jersey track suit are better options than the shiny styles if your figure is less than perfect.

On the topic of the eye being drawn to sheen and shine, remember that belt buckles also can often be shiny objects. If you don't want too much attention on your waistline but need to wear a belt,

Above: Horizontal lines, shiny fabrics, light colours are shortening and widening

Right: Vertical lines, matt fabrics, dark colours are lengthening and slimming

fabric- or leather-covered buckles can be more flattering than shiny metal ones.

Colour

The colours next to your face which will work best for your individual colouring can be found in Chapter 4, but it is also useful to know that dark colours (black, navy, brown, burgundy, pine green and so on) act rather like matt fabrics in that they absorb the light and make areas appear smaller. Yes, that's why women always go on about black being slimming – it's not a myth! If, however, the black garment is made of a shiny fabric such as black nylon it will no longer be slimming, because the power of the shine over-rides the power of the colour. So if you want to reduce certain areas of your body, deep coloured matt fabrics will always be best. Every man can wear dark suits, trousers, jackets and coats if they are teamed with a 'personal' colour near the face in the form of a shirt, sweater or tie.

Lighter colours (cream, beige, taupe, stone, dove-grey and so on) have more reflective qualities and therefore make areas appear larger. If you have to choose between chinos in cream or navy and are worried about the size of your rear, opt for the navy pair every time! Simply wear them with a better shade for your colouring near your face for a flattering effect.

Scale

The final bit of trickery that our eyes can play on our brain is in connection with differing sizes and scales of objects. Nothing is viewed in isolation – only in relation to what is surrounding it. Look at the diagram opposite and assess which central blob is the bigger – the one above or the one below?

In fact, both central blobs are the same size. The one at the top appears larger because it is surrounded by small objects; the one at the bottom appears smaller because it is surrounded by large objects. So how does this affect your appearance? Quite simply, if you are a big man (very tall, overweight or large-boned), very small details such as a skinny tie with a small knot or tiny patterns or small jewellery, will actually make you look larger. A very short, thin or small-boned man who opts for very large

Below: Which central blob is the biggest?

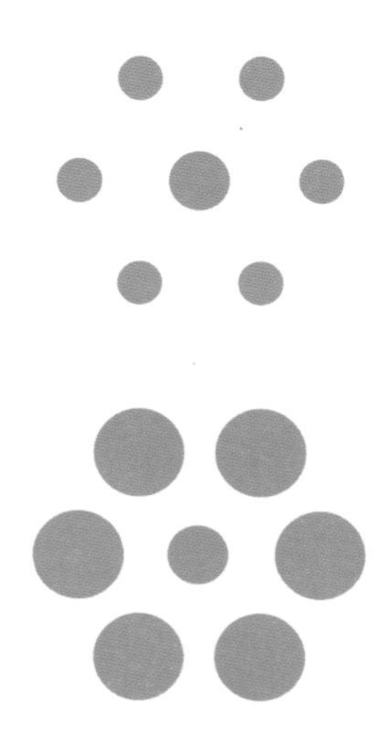

Above: A big man needs large scale patterns (e.g. check shirt) and large accessories (e.g. watch) to project an aura of confidence about who and what he is.

patterns, a wide tie and huge jewellery can easily be swamped and overpowered and ultimately look smaller than he actually is.

A large man needs larger-scale accessories and patterns, firstly for them to be in keeping with his size and secondly to project an aura of confidence about who and what he is. A short man will often try to make himself look bigger with a large briefcase or watch, but small to average pieces are in fact needed to increase his degree of professionalism and credibility.

Figure Proportions

Armed with your knowledge of line, fabric, colour and scale, you may be able to start working out how to highlight or diminish your good and not-so-good bits and pieces. But first study the list below and tick the boxes for your particular proportions. You don't need to put a tick for all the body areas listed. For example, if your neck is neither long nor short, or if your shoulders are neither too narrow nor too wide, just ignore these boxes and concentrate on the areas which you want to deal with:

☐ Short/thick neck	☐ Long/thin neck
☐ Narrow shoulders	☐ Broad shoulders
☐ Too tall/very long legs	☐ Too short/very short legs
☐ Beer belly	☐ Big bottom

Short or thick neck

Go for:

Lower necklines (e.g. V-neck)
Shirts with a narrow collar band (or none) connecting collar to body of shirt
Slightly longer shirt collar
Spread collar
Open collar for casual wear
The clean-shaven look
Discreet ties

Open neckline

Avoid:

Polo-necks
Turtle-necks
Cravats
'Loud' ties
Contrasting collars
Beards
Buttoned-up necklines

Buttoned-up neckline

Long or skinny neck

Go for:

- Higher necklines
- Shirts with a wide band connecting collar to body of shirt
- Short points on shirt collar
- Slightly wider tie
- Turtle- or polo-necks
- Contrasting collars on casual wear
- Shirts buttoned at neck for casual wear
- Beard

Polo neck

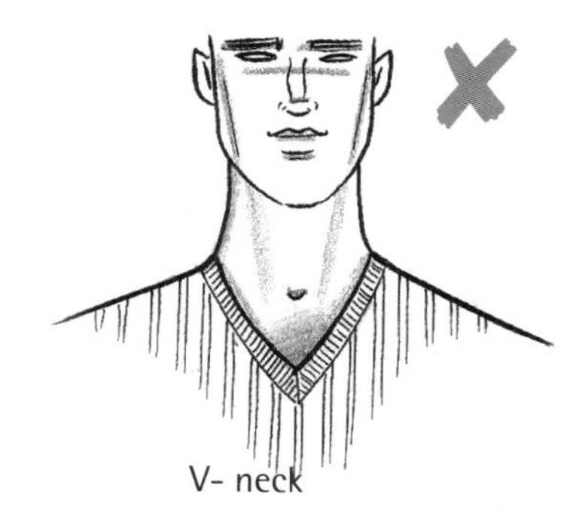

V- neck

Avoid:

- V-neck sweaters (worn alone)
- Shirts open at neckline
- Long pointed collars
- Very narrow ties

Narrow shoulders

Go for:

- Fuller shoulder pads in jackets
- Horizontal details on tops
- Checks on jackets
- Bulky knit sweaters
- Loose-fitting tops
- Dropped shoulder seams

Horizontal details

Raglan sleeves

Avoid:

- V-necklines
- Raglan sleeves
- Vertical stripes on tops
- Tight-fitting tops
- Light, shiny shirts
- Fine knitwear

Broad shoulders

Go for:

- V-necklines
- Raglan sleeves
- Vertical details
- Tight-fitting tops
- Light shiny tops
- Fine knitwear

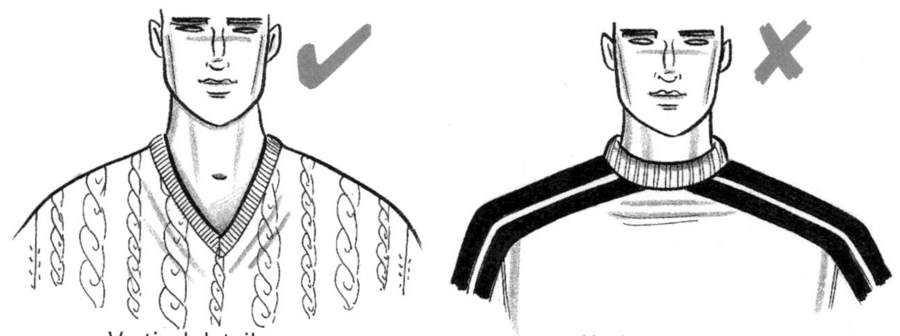

Vertical details

Horizontal details

Avoid:

- Excessive shoulder padding
- Horizontal details
- Check jackets
- Bulky knits
- Loose, baggy tops
- Dropped shoulder seams

Too short (or very short legs)

Go for:

Jackets that just cover seat with no extra length
Vertical patterns
High-rise trousers
Single-breasted jackets
Pin-stripe suits
Straight-leg trousers
Slightly narrow tie
Blended colours (e.g. charcoal jacket, black trousers)

Avoid:

Turn-ups
Strong contrast between sports jacket/blazer and trousers
Check trousers/jackets
Double-breasted jackets
Wide-leg trousers
Pleats on waistband
Wide waistbands/belts

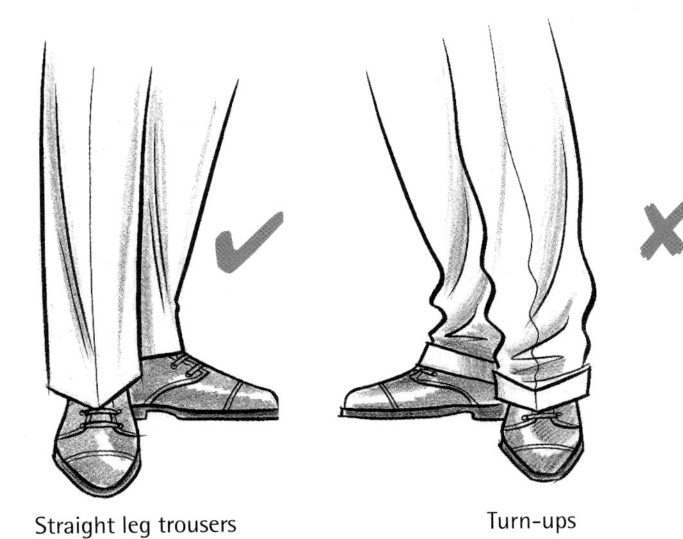

Straight leg trousers

Turn-ups

Too tall (or over-long legs)

Go for:

Long-line jackets
Double-breasted jackets
Contrasting colour for blazer/sports jacket and trousers
Horizontal stripes (sweaters etc.)
Turn-ups on trousers
Wide belts
Trousers low on waist
Check or patterned trousers/shorts
Pleats on trousers

Avoid:

High-rise trousers
High-closure single-breasted jackets
Narrow belts
Pin-stripe suits
Vertical patterns
Very thin ties
Very short jackets

Checks and turn-ups

High rise and pinstripes

Beer belly

Go for:

Loosely fitted clothes

Trousers above stomach (braces may be needed)

Wider tie ending at top of belt

Trousers that hang straight down from bottom

Vertical lines on tops

Little contrast between jacket and trousers

Waistcoat with suit

Single-breasted jackets

Avoid:

Tightly fitted clothes

Pleated trousers

Wearing trousers under stomach

Checks or horizontals on tops

Double-breasted styles

Narrow ties or too short ties

Contrast between jacket and trousers

Vertical stripes/ribs

Checks/or horizontals

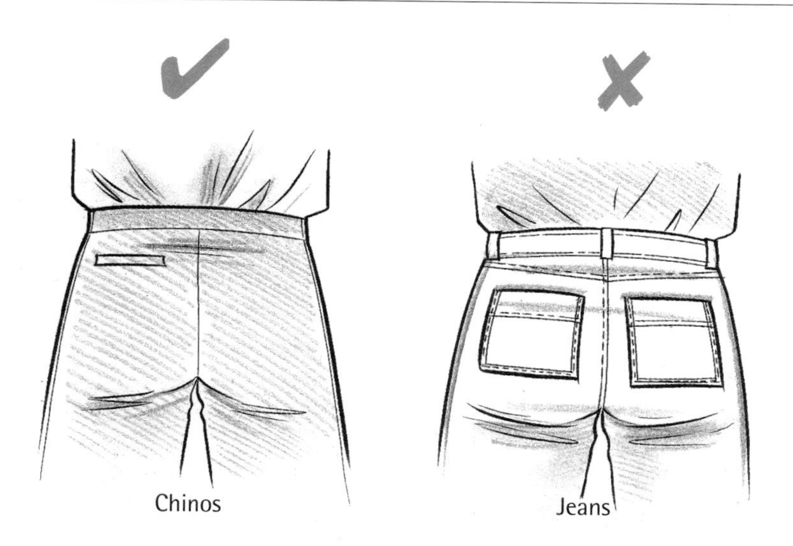

Chinos

Jeans

Big bum

Go for:

Trousers/shorts in dark colours

Chino-style casual trousers

Few pockets

Matt fabrics

Good fit at waistline

Avoid:

Trousers in light colours

Too many pockets on trousers (e.g. jeans)

Shiny fabrics

Check patterns

Low-slung trousers/shorts

N.B. Should the advice given for one proportion conflict with that given for another, take the advice for the proportion that causes most problems.

Chapter 4

Colour Directions

Working out which colours suit you, or 'having your colours done' became a big industry in the 1970s and 1980s, particularly for women who wanted an easy guide through the maze of fashion and cosmetic colours which faced them each season. If you have a wife or girlfriend, you are probably familiar with the scenario whereby the woman stands in front of her bulging wardrobe (with the EU shoe mountain growing at the bottom) and each day declares, 'I've nothing to wear!' before dressing for work or an evening out. The colour analysis industry arose out of the need for women to develop planned, organized wardrobes based around their best 'personal' colours so that they could 'mix and match' their garments and produce lots of different outfits out of relatively fewer clothes.

Above: Understanding your Colour Direction can help you select colours to complement or contrast with your colouring for your desired effect.

Colour Moves into the Business World

As a man, you're probably thinking, 'Well, I don't wear make-up and I don't have a problem putting an outfit together in the morning, so how can colour analysis help me?' Quite simply, the colours you wear have a big effect on how others perceive you and relate to you. During the early 1990s, the colour analysis industry began to move into the business sector, as it was realized not only that women (and business-women in particular) who had experienced colour analysis had more planned, flexible wardrobes, but that their new coordinated appearance gave them more confidence, more presence, more credibility and ultimately an edge over their colleagues. It is now quite common practice for companies or individuals (particularly those in the public eye such as politicians, TV presenters and sportsmen) to hire the services of image consultants to ensure that colours being worn, used as backgrounds on platforms or in studios, and on corporate literature and brochures are all giving out the right message to the viewer.

Colour: Some Facts

Before we look at which colours are best for the message you wish to relay to the world, here's some background information about colour which will demonstrate that the advice you will be given is based in fact rather than fantasy.

It was in the seventeenth century that Sir Isaac Newton discovered the visible spectrum – what we see as the rainbow – and mapped how light breaks into wavelengths of radiant energy. Because colour is a vibrational movement like sound, colours exist which we humans cannot perceive – just as there are sounds which a dog hears but we cannot. Many people believe that our sensitivity to colour perception is on the increase, and that we may in future see colours not recognized by our eyes today.

As colour is an energy wave we also 'feel' it although we are not consciously aware of this happening. Some blind people, however, whose other senses are heightened to compensate for their lack of sight, can actually tell the difference between colours by touch. So your brain is affected daily by the different energies of colours you see and feel – your mood, appetite, body functions, concentration, creativity and energy levels can all be affected by the colour of the walls! Similarly, your own colouring and the colours you choose to wear will be having an effect on other people.

Red

The longest ray in the visible spectrum, red makes the biggest impact on the retina – in other words we 'see' it before all other colours. Football teams with red strips will also see their team-mates a fraction of a second before those in other strips, which can be crucial to accurate passing of the ball. Red also raises blood pressure, quickens the pulse and rate of breathing, and leads to feelings of aggression or agitation.

Blue

By contrast, blue slows down body activity and stimulates the mind. It's a good colour for classrooms or studies, but not good for a sports changing room where red would be more effective. Blue also stifles the appetite (there are no naturally coloured

bright blue foods), so if you want to diet and eat less serve your food on blue plates to make you feel less hungry. Blueberries and juniper berries are closer to purple than blue.

Orange

This colour is the biggest appetite stimulant, which is why it is used widely by fast-food chains such as McDonald's. Children will eat most foods which are orange – fish fingers, carrots, orange juice – because their brains are stimulated by the colour.

Above: A soft shade of green makes your bedroom a restful, relaxing place of calm - or paint it red (left) to evoke feelings of passion, appetite and energy!

If you remove the orange breadcrumbs from fish fingers, they will refuse them; if you dye brussels sprouts orange with food dye, they will eat them!

Green

Because it gives off feelings of calm and relaxation, green is often used for doctor's or hospital waiting rooms, where you will sit patiently for your overdue appointment without becoming agitated or aggressive. After blue, it is the second most unappetizing colour – hence children's gut-reaction dislike of green vegetables. As an adult you learn to over-ride your feelings because education tells you that greens are good for you.

Characteristics of Colour

So colour is a vibration having profound effects on our eyes and brain and, because it is an energy wave like sound, it is capable of reflection, diffraction and interference. In music, the physical phenomena of intensity, frequency and wave-form create our perception of loudness, pitch and tone; in colour the same physical phenomena create our perception of depth, clarity and undertone.

Depth

This is how deep or light a colour is. For example, charcoal-grey is deep and dove-grey is light. They are simply different intensities of the same colour (with many other depths of grey in between). It is important to remember that 'deep' does not mean 'dark'; 'deep' means 'strong' and 'intense'. Fuchsia pink is a deep colour (but it is definitely not dark), whilst baby pink is a light intensity of the same colour. In fact, light colours are simply a diluted version of deeper colours – a small drop of fuchsia pink paint stirred into a glass of water would result in the baby pink shade.

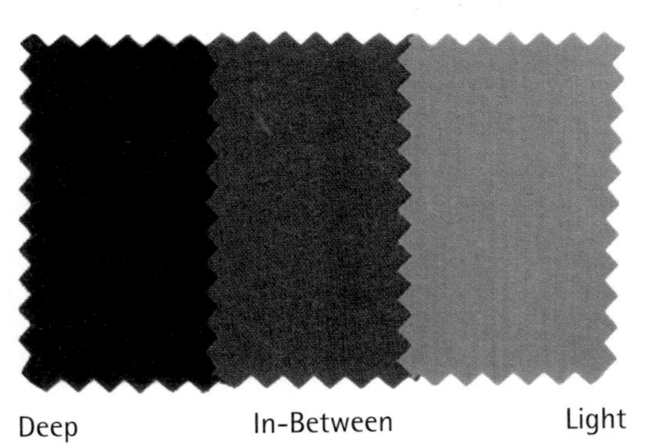

Deep In-Between Light

Clarity

This is how bright or muted a colour is. For example, lime green is bright and sage green is muted. A bright colour is clear and vivid and reaches the eye very quickly because of its sharpness. A muted colour is soft and subtle and reaches the eye quite slowly because of its greyish, cloudy composition. Returning to our paint analogy, to turn a bright paint into a muted one you would add quantities of grey paint to lessen the clear, sharp, vivid qualities.

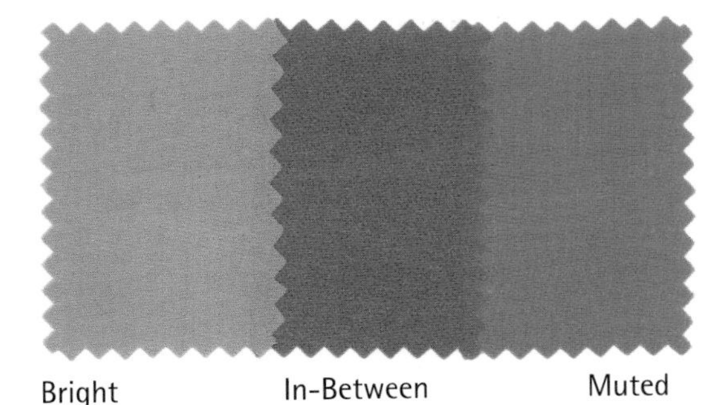

Bright In-Between Muted

Undertone

This is how cool or warm a colour is. For example, blood red is a cool red and tomato red is a warm red. What makes a colour warm or cool is varying amounts of yellow or blue within its composition. All colours contain both yellow and blue, but in differing degrees which are not always visible to the human eye. Colours with a lot of yellow (for example orange, tan and peach) are warm colours; colours with a lot of blue (for example black, fuchsia and purple) are cool colours. To make a colour warmer you would add yellow; to make it cooler you would add blue.

Warm In-Between Cool

Discovering Your Colour Direction

Personal Characteristics

Having some understanding of colour means that you can apply the above characteristics and basic terminology to yourself, because your skin, hair and eyes are all made up of pigments or colours. Melanin is a brown pigment found in skin, hair and eyes. Carotene is a yellow-orange pigment also found in skin, hair and eyes. Haemoglobin is a bluey red pigment in blood and is sometimes visible through the skin.

The system which I use to determine colours for individuals, called Colour Directions, is extremely flexible. It helps you to understand your most harmonious colours, but also explains the effects that other colours will have with your colouring if you want to achieve a different look either all the time or just on certain occasions. Also, the Colour Direction that you are now is not necessarily how you will stay forever. As we get older our skin, hair and eyes all fade as pigment is lost, so our colouring can change naturally from one Colour Direction to another. If you decide to colour your hair or wear coloured contact lenses your Colour Direction will almost definitely change, but the system is flexible enough to guide you as changes occur – naturally or otherwise.

On the chart opposite you will probably find that one category is much easier to

DIY Colour Analysis

To discover your Colour Direction, look at yourself in the mirror and tick three boxes below – one for depth, one for clarity and one for undertone.

The DEPTH of my colouring is best described as:

- ☐ Deep, strong, intense
- ☐ Light, fair, soft
- ☐ Don't know or somewhere in between

The CLARITY of my colouring is best described as:

- ☐ Bright, vivid, contrasting
- ☐ Muted, subtle, non-contrasting
- ☐ Don't know or somewhere in between

The UNDERTONE of my colouring is best described as:

- ☐ Warm, golden, burnished
- ☐ Cool, silvery, ashy
- ☐ Don't know or somewhere in between

tick than the other two. For example, a fair-skinned man with blonde hair and blue eyes will tick box 2 without hesitation but may think long and hard about all the other alternatives. A dark-skinned man with black hair and brown eyes will tick box 1 easily but probably ponder some other choices. A freckly-skinned redhead with green eyes will tick box 6 without any qualms but perhaps query his selections in the earlier choices. This is quite normal, because it tells you something very important about your colouring – *whichever box was easiest to tick is probably your Primary Colour Direction.* If you found two boxes easy to tick, you've probably discovered your Secondary Colour Direction too – all you need now is to put them in the right order.

To put your Colour Directions in order of importance, draw an illustration like the one opposite, putting crosses where you feel your answers to the questions fall. Use pencil at first, as you may change your mind after some thought.

Can't Decide?

If you couldn't decide between your Primary and Secondary Colour Direction or if (yes, it does happen occasionally) you answered 'don't know' in all the categories, look at the pictures and descriptions on the following pages to find the colouring which most closely resembles your own. You will then be able to discover your most harmonious clothing colours for next to your face (jackets, shirts, ties and so on) and even colours for spectacle frames to complete the picture.

I have stressed that colours only need to be harmonious next to the face. On your body, style, shape and fit of clothing are more important. Any man can wear a navy suit, but a Light man might want to team it with an ivory shirt, for instance; a Cool man with a white shirt; and a Warm man with a cream shirt.

You can, if you choose, wear your harmonious colours from head to toe, and the look will be great if the style is also right for you. Remember, however, that where colour is concerned you have the freedom to go with your own tastes or follow fashion trends on the major part of your body, if you so wish. For this reason I only include card swatches in my mail-order makeover service, as I don't want men to see swatches as expensive 'bibles' containing the only

Do-It-Yourself Colour Analysis – Have a Go!

DEPTH

1.DEEP (Strong/Intense) — 2. LIGHT (Fair, Soft)

Very	Slightly	Don't know/In-between	Slightly	Very
				✗

CLARITY

3. BRIGHT (Vivid, Contrasting) — 4. MUTED (Subtle, Non-Contrasting)

Very	Slightly	Don't know/In-between	Slightly	Very
			✗	

UNDERTONE

5. COOL (Cool, Ashy) — 6. WARM (Golden, Burnished)

Very	Slightly	Don't know/In-between	Slightly	Very
		✗		

The crosses shown on the chart above are the answers for the man pictured right. With blonde hair, blue eyes and a fair complexion, box 2 is his easiest to tick, so Light is his Primary Colour Direction. His colouring is subtle, with very little contrast, so box 4 is the next easiest to tick, making Muted his Secondary Colour Direction. As he has golden blonde hair (warm), blue eyes (cool) and skin which is rosy in winter (cool) and freckly in summer (warm), Undertone is therefore not important to him – he can wear both warm and cool colours. What is most important is that his most harmonious colours are Light and his second best are Muted.

colours that they can wear. You don't need to take the card on every shopping trip or try to 'match' it to every garment in the shop. Colour Analysis has moved on from the days when a swatch was regarded as a necessary crutch. Today, with Colour Directions you simply understand your colouring and consequently know how to shop for the effect you want to achieve. Study the advice for your own Colour Directions in the following pages.

Deep Direction

(e.g. Seve Ballesteros, Sylvester Stallone, Frank Bruno)

This colour pattern is the most common throughout the world, particularly in hot climates, and is often described as **strong**, *powerful* or intense. Most black or Asian men will have *deep* as their Primary Colour Direction unless they have coloured their hair, wear coloured contact lenses or have gone grey.

Typical Colourings

Hair: black, dark to mid-brown, chestnut brown (not red).

Eyes: dark brown, deep hazel, olive green, dark blue.

Skin tone: medium to dark (often tans easily).

Harmonious Colours

Jackets/suits: black, charcoal, dark brown, deep navy, olive.

Formal shirts: white, icy blue, icy pink, lilac, mint.

Ties/casual jackets/sweaters etc.: true red, pine green, purple, royal blue, burgundy, deep turquoise, rust, terracotta.

Fashion colours each season: any deep, strong, intense colours will suit you well.

Glasses frames: dark brown, black, charcoal, tortoiseshell, dark metals.

Secondary Colour Direction

(another Colour Direction can be added to your palette)

- If you are Deep but have lots of contrast between your dark hair/eye colour and a lighter skin tone, your Secondary Colour Direction is **Bright** (see p.78).
- If you are Deep and have mid-brown hair, medium skin tone and medium-depth eyes, your Secondary Colour Direction is **Muted** (see p.80).
- If you are Deep but have evidence of blue/ashy tones, your Secondary Colour Direction is **Cool** (see p.84).
- If you are Deep but have evidence of golden tones, your Secondary Colour Direction is **Warm** (see p.82).

Above: Deep blues and reds together with pure white are great for casual wear.

Right: Deep colouring can take the intensity of a matching dark shirt and tie.

Opposite Colour Direction

Light (see p.76) is your opposite Colour Direction. Pale colours such as pink, blue, beige, cream and lemon are the most difficult colours for you to wear, especially near the face or in glasses frames. If you do wear light shades they will give you a non-harmonious, contrasting look. If you are quite extrovert or like a high-fashion look they can be eye-catching and extreme, but they need a lot of style or confidence to carry off well.

Light Direction

(e.g. Prince William, Paul Hogan, Ronan Keating)

This colour pattern is very common in the Western world, particularly England and Scandinavia, and can be described as soft or fair. These men can easily be overpowered by very dark colours near the face, particularly in business-wear, which only serve to highlight their 'light' look.

Above: A deep colour next to your face will give a contrasting, high fashion look.

Far left: Light shirt and tie colours will complement your colouring.

Typical Colourings

Hair: golden blond, ash blond, very light brown/mousy, yellow grey.

Eye colour: blue, green, grey, blue/grey, green/blue.

Skin tone: medium to light (often does not tan easily).

Harmonious Colours

Jackets/Suits: light grey, light navy, taupe, camel, stone.

Formal shirts: ivory, lemon, pale pink, peach, pastel blue.

Ties/casual jackets/sweaters etc.: denim blue, violet, coral, watermelon red, light turquoise, aqua, sage green, dusky pink.

Fashion colours each season: any light to medium colours will suit you well.

Glasses frames: light metals, pale grey, taupe, frameless.

Secondary Colour Direction

(another Colour Direction can be added to your palette)

- If you are Light but have bright eyes and/or extremely blond hair, your Secondary Colour Direction is **Bright** (see p.78).
- If you are Light but have cloudy/pale eyes and subtle blond hair, your Secondary Colour Direction is **Muted** (see p.80).
- If you are Light but have evidence of bluey/ashy tones, your Secondary Colour Direction is **Cool** (see p.84).
- If you are Light but have considerable evidence of golden/yellowy tones, your Secondary Colour Direction is **Warm** (see p.82).

Opposite Colour Direction

Deep (see p.74) is your opposite Colour Direction. Strong, intense colours such as burgundy, bright red, black, bottle green and deep purple are the most difficult for you to wear, especially near the face or as glasses frames. If you do wear Deep shades, they will give you a non-harmonious, contrasting look. If you are quite extrovert or like a high-fashion look they can be eye-catching and extreme, but they need a lot of style or confidence to carry off well.

Bright Direction

(e.g. Hugh Grant, Michael Douglas, Richard E. Grant)

This colour pattern is characterized by a contrast between hair, skin and eyes – usually dark hair with a light skin and bright eye. It is often described as *sharp*, *vivid* or *clear*. As a natural colour pattern it is often found in men with Celtic origins, particularly the Irish, who are famous for their 'twinkling eyes'.

Typical Colourings

Hair: black, medium to dark brown, chestnut (can be grey or blond only if brows are dark).

Eyes: bright blue, green, turquoise, bright hazel, violet (jewel-like).

Skin tone: light to medium (may tan or burn)

Above: Bright colours, together with black and white are great for your casual wear.

Far right: Bright colouring can take the contrast of a dark shirt and light satin tie.

Harmonious Colours

Jackets/suits: charcoal, dark brown, bright navy, black.

Formal shirts: pure white, icy blue, warm pink, lilac, lemon.

Ties/casual jackets/sweaters etc.: scarlet red, bright pink, lime green, electric blue, coral, bright turquoise, emerald, violet.

Fashion colours each season: any bright, clear, sharp colours will suit you well.

Glasses frames: black, charcoal, dark brown, shiny metals (bright frames when in fashion).

Secondary Colour Direction

(another Colour Direction can be added to your palette)

- If you are Bright and have dark brown hair and brows, your Secondary Colour Direction is **Deep** (see p.74).
- If you are Bright and have mid-brown hair and brows, your Secondary Colour Direction is **Light** (see p.76).
- If you are Bright and have evidence of bluey/ashy tones, your Secondary Colour Direction is **Cool** (see p.84).
- If you are Bright and have evidence of golden/yellowy tones, your Secondary Colour Direction is **Warm** (see p.82).

Opposite Colour Direction

Muted dusky shades such as beige, sage green, dusky pink, mustard and powder blue are the most difficult for you to wear, especially near the face or as glasses frames. If you do wear muted shades they will detract from your sharp, bright look. If you are quite extrovert or if you like a high-fashion look they can be eye-catching and extreme, but they need a lot of style or confidence to carry off well.

Muted Direction

(e.g. Brad Pitt, Rod Stewart, Paddy Ashdown)

This colour pattern is quite unusual in adults – most dark-eyed men also have dark hair, and lighter hair may be the result of sun exposure or bleach. The resulting colouring is often described as *mellow*, *rich* or *subtle*. Blond hair with a dark eye colour does not provide a sharp contrast (as with dark hair and a light eye) but gives a more blended look.

Typical Colourings

Hair: blond, light brown/mousy, yellow grey.

Eyes: brown, hazel, olive green, greeny/grey.

Skin tone: medium to deep (may tan or burn).

Harmonious Colours

Jackets/suits: bronzed grey, muted navy, taupe, olive, coffee.

Formal shirts: cream, off-white, beige, lemon, peach, pale green.

Ties/casual jackets/sweaters etc.: rust, mahogany, khaki green, tomato red, gold, dusky pink, teal, purple.

Fashion colours each season: any muted, soft, rich, blended colours will suit you well.

Glasses frames: beige, brown, soft grey, tortoiseshell, brushed metals.

Secondary Colour Directions

(another Colour Direction can be added to your palette)

- If you are Muted and have light brown hair and brown eyes, your Secondary Colour Direction is **Deep** (see p.74).
- If you are Muted and have light hair and light hazel eyes, your Secondary Colour Direction is **Light** (see p.76).
- If you are Muted and have evidence of bluey/ashy tones, your Secondary Colour Direction is **Cool** (see p.84).
- If you are Muted and have evidence of golden/yellowy tones, your Secondary Colour Direction is **Warm** (see p.82).

Right: Select ties with soft, mellow colours for your business look.

Left: Grey, beige and stone are ideal neutrals for your wardrobe.

Opposite Colour Direction

Bright, sharp, clear colours such as fuchsia pink, pure white, emerald green and scarlet are the most difficult for you to wear, especially near the face or for glasses frames. If you do wear bright shades they can be overpowering to your subtle look. If you are quite extrovert or if you like a high-fashion look they can be eye-catching and extreme, but they need a lot of style or confidence to carry them off well.

Warm Direction

(e.g. Boris Becker, Chris Evans, Kenneth Branagh)

This *golden, burnished, fiery* colour pattern is often associated in its natural state with northern countries, particularly Scotland. It is caused by an abundance of the pigment carotene in the hair and eyes, and often in the skin as freckles. It is men with this colouring who find it most difficult to wear the traditional corporate look of a 'cool' suit (navy or grey) and white shirt – business clothes should be chosen with care.

Typical Colourings

Hair: red, auburn, copper, ginger, sandy/strawberry.

Eyes: brown, hazel, bright blue/turquoise, green.

Skin tone: golden or very pale (often burns easily and may have freckles).

Harmonious Colours

Jackets/suits: warm navy, medium grey, brown, olive, camel.

Formal shirts: ivory, peach, beige, yellow, green.

Ties/casual jackets/sweaters etc.: teal, turquoise, terracotta, rust, orange, tomato red, gold, jade, aqua, bronze.

Fashion colours each season: any warm, golden, fiery or burnished colours will suit you well.

Glasses frames: brown, tortoiseshell, beige, golden metals.

Secondary Colour Direction

(another Colour Direction can be added to your palette)

- If you are Warm and have dark red hair and dark eyes, your Secondary Colour Direction is **Deep** (see p.74).
- If you are Warm and have light red hair and light eyes, your Secondary Colour Direction is **Light** (see p.76).
- If you are Warm and have bright red/ginger hair or bright blue/green eyes, your Secondary Colour Direction is **Bright** (see p.78).
- If you are Warm and have light red hair with darker eyes, your Secondary Colour Direction is **Muted** (see p.80).

Above: Green, brown, rust and khaki are ideal colours for your casual wardrobe.

Right: Select ties with warm golden colours when wearing grey or navy suits.

Opposite Colour Direction

Cool, icy or bluey colours such as white, ice blue, pale pink, fuchsia and lilac are the most difficult for you to wear – especially near the face or for glasses frames. If you do wear cool shades they will give you a non-harmonious, contrasting look. If you are quite extrovert or if you like a high-fashion look they can be eye-catching and extreme, but they need a lot of style or confidence to carry off well.

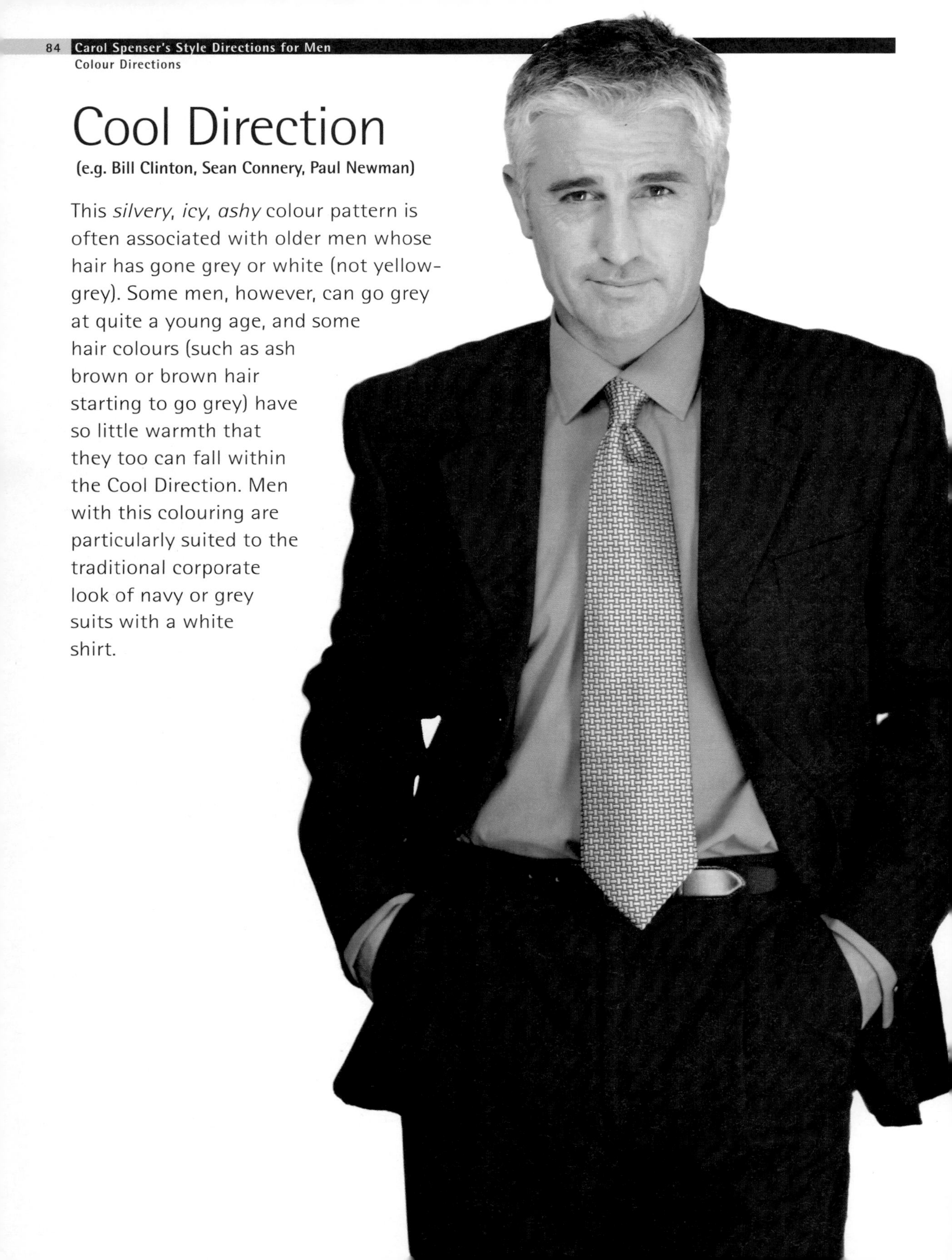

Cool Direction

(e.g. Bill Clinton, Sean Connery, Paul Newman)

This *silvery, icy, ashy* colour pattern is often associated with older men whose hair has gone grey or white (not yellow-grey). Some men, however, can go grey at quite a young age, and some hair colours (such as ash brown or brown hair starting to go grey) have so little warmth that they too can fall within the Cool Direction. Men with this colouring are particularly suited to the traditional corporate look of navy or grey suits with a white shirt.

Typical Colourings

Hair: white, steely grey, ash/greyish brown.

Eyes: blue, blue/grey, greyish brown.

Skin tone: pale, rosy or ashy (very few freckles); can be deeper if eyes are brown.

Harmonious Colours

Jackets/suits: any grey, any navy, taupe, stone.

Formal shirts: white, icy pink, icy blue, lilac, mint.

Ties/casual jackets/sweater etc.: blue-reds, royal blue, purple, plum, fuchsia pink, denim blue, pine green, emerald, turquoise, rose pink.

Fashion colours each season: any cool, icy or bluey colours will suit you well.

Glasses frames: silver, grey, black, gunmetal, blue.

Secondary Colour Direction

(another Colour Direction can be added to your palette)

- If you are Cool and have darker hair and eyes, your Secondary Colour Direction is **Deep** (see p.74).
- If you are Cool and have light hair and eyes, your Secondary Colour Direction is **Light** (see p.76).
- If you are Cool and have lots of contrast in your colouring (for instance bright eyes and dark brows), your Secondary Colour Direction is **Bright** (see p.78).
- If you are Cool and have light hair with darker eyes, your Secondary Colour Direction is **Muted** (see p.80).

Above: When wearing neutrals(navy , grey, black etc.) use white as a contrast colour to prevent a monotone look.

Left: Blue, pink or lilac shirts are perfect for cool colouring.

Opposite Colour Direction

Warm, golden or yellowy colours such as orange, lime green, egg yellow and tan are the most difficult for you to wear, especially near the face or for glasses frames. If you do wear warm shades they will give you a non-harmonious, contrasting look. If you are quite extrovert or if you like a high-fashion look they can be eye-catching and extreme, but they need a lot of style and confidence to carry off well.

Chapter 5

Grooming Directions

The field of men's grooming products is now one of the fastest growing segments of the skincare and toiletries market. Until the mid-1990s, however, most skincare products were aimed predominantly at women – men traditionally lavished more loving care and attention on their car bodywork than on their own skin! A typically male skincare routine consisted of a quick daily shave with a sharp razor and shaving cream or soap, swiftly followed by the ritual splashing of a stinging after-shave on raw skin. In past decades, advertisements for aftershave always featured rugged sportsmen – boxers, footballers or yachtsmen – to reassure the male user that this was a 'macho' product and in no way associated with 'girlie' perfume or any other 'feminine' skin preparations. But things have changed dramatically over the past few years.

As we enter a new millennium, today's man is much more interested in taking care of his skin and will be either buying his own skincare products or borrowing those of his partner – with or without her knowledge. If you fall into the latter category, it's time you started to make some room in the bathroom cabinet for a range of skincare products specifically designed to meet the needs of a man's skin. Just as you may have a preference for a particular brand of deodorant or shampoo, it's important to find the right grooming products for your skin.

Above: Regular skin and hair care routines are just as important to looking and feeling good as having the right clothes.

Male Versus Female Skin

So let's begin with the basics and take a close look at what makes men's skin different from that of women. It isn't the *structure*, which is basically identical regardless of sex, race and age. The skin consists of three layers: the subdermis, dermis and epidermis.

- The **sub-dermis** is a layer of fatty tissue that cushions the skin above it.
- The **dermis** is the middle layer of skin. It contains collagen (the body's super-protein that gives skin bounce) and elastin (the substance that gives skin flexibility and

The Structure of the Skin

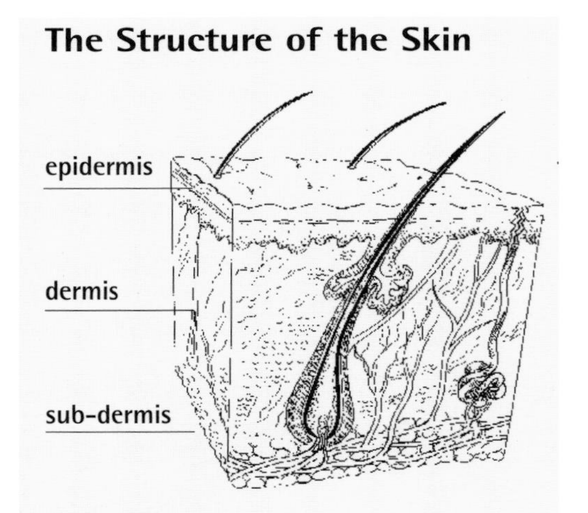

durability). The dermis also contains blood capillaries, nerves, hair follicles, sweat and sebaceous (oil) glands.

- The **epidermis** is the top layer of skin. It is only 1/250 of an inch thick (that's about a tenth of a millimetre) and performs the critical function of cell renewal, which is what keeps your skin young and healthy-looking.

Although the structure of male and female skin is the same, there are some notable differences in its physiology. Firstly, men's skin is thicker because it contains more of the supporting fibres, elastin and collagen. Also, its tendency to produce more sebum (a result of the male hormone androgen) makes it oilier and, along with the typically larger pore size, explains why men (and male adolescents in particular) are more likely to suffer from acne. Sebaceous glands in men are active right up to the age of eighty or so, whereas a woman's skin tends to become increasingly dry as she gets older, especially around the menopause.

The other major difference between a man's skin and a woman's is, of course, the development of facial hair and the fact that most men shave it off day after day. In fact, the average male will spend around 150 days of his life shaving off almost 30 feet (10 metres) of beard. It is this unremitting daily routine which places added stress on a man's skin and creates the requirement for specialized male products. Although shaving can act as a good exfoliator (getting rid of old, dead skin cells) it also causes problems such as an unpleasant, tight sensation and dry, flaky skin, because the face is being deprived of essential substances called lipids which retain moisture.

Shaving may also lead, in some cases, to razor burn – a red rash which often appears under the chin and on the neck. Or it can cause ingrown hairs which produce painful raised lumps. Small wonder then, that as many as 40 per cent of men believe they suffer from sensitive skin – a far greater percentage than women! Also, because shaving removes both dead and living cells from the skin's surface, it leaves younger cells more exposed to the detrimental effects of the environment or a stressful lifestyle.

External Factors Affecting Your Skin

Shaving every day leaves new 'raw' skin exposed to the following:

Sun Possibly the most damaging of environmental factors is the sun. Its rays stimulate the skin's production of vitamin D, providing a feeling of warmth and well-being and often a deceptively healthy-looking tan. However, over the years continued exposure to the sun's ultraviolet rays will dry out, damage and wrinkle the skin considerably. The rise in the incidence of skin cancer is now, also, among the fastest of any type of cancer in the world.

Humidity Low humidity, often caused by heating systems in houses, offices and cars, robs the skin of essential moisture. High humidity, on the other hand, can cause the sweat glands to work overtime, making the skin feel oily. But even though your skin may feel oilier in hot and humid weather, it still needs moisturizing to guard against the detrimental effects of the sun.

Temperature Cold temperatures, combined with low humidity, increase moisture loss from the skin, leaving it tight and dry. Hot temperatures combined with low humidity also remove moisture from the surface, literally 'baking' the skin. Extreme heat and cold can, therefore, both damage the skin.

Wind Strong wind, especially when combined with extreme temperatures and low humidity, can cause dry and flaky skin. Also, wind-borne dust and dirt can strike the skin and stick to its surface, clogging the pores and choking the skin.

Pollution Smog and other pollutants can stick to the skin, clogging up the pores. Men who live and work in densely populated, industrial towns and cities with heavy traffic need to protect their skin from the damaging effects of pollution.

Left: Skin cancer is one of the fastest growing cancers in the world today, particularly among men. Always use SPF products and cover up with a loose shirt at the hottest times of the day.

Lifestyle Factors Affecting Your Skin

Controlling wind, humidity, temperature and pollution is often beyond our personal control – all we can do is use the best products available to combat those elements. Some factors affecting our skin are, however, totally within our control and can make a huge difference to our skin's health and appearance.

Sleep This is the simplest and most basic remedy for skin. During sleep, our skin renews itself by building new cells, so getting the proper amount of sleep each night is essential. Seven to eight hours a night is recommended for healthy-looking skin.

Water The body needs fluid to flush out impurities. Drinking six to eight glasses of water (about 1 1/2 – 2 litres) per day can help to improve the circulation and speed cell growth. Drinking plenty of water also (paradoxically) helps prevent water retention and bloating and can help with weight loss.

Nutrition Food provides all the vitamins and minerals the body needs to function properly. There is a direct correlation between healthy skin and good nutrition, so it is extremely important to eat a balanced and healthy diet. An unbalanced diet will often result in poor skin, which is also a reflection of the poor condition of other unseen organs.

Exercise Regular exercise helps the circulation and speeds the blood to the surface of the skin to help regenerate it. Not only do you immediately look better after exercise, with a healthy glow, but the long-term effects can be rejuvenating. Exercise can also alleviate the negative effects of stress.

Stress blemishes, hives ('nettle-rash' lumps), loss of colour and dark circles under the eyes can all be caused by stress. Having a constantly tense expression can also permanently line your face. Practise relaxing your facial muscles in order to avoid frowning or furrowing your brow when under stress.

Toxic Substances Nicotine, alcohol, caffeine and other drugs can be the skin's worst enemies. Smoking constricts the blood vessels in the face, allowing less blood, oxygen and nutrients to reach the surface of the skin and therefore making it look older. Alcohol and caffeine are diuretics that force moisture out of your system and dry out your skin; if your intake of alcohol or caffeine is high on a particular day, drink plenty of water the following day to rehydrate your body, especially the skin.

Right: Regular exercise improves circulation which results in increased blood supply to the skin and a look of healthy well-being.

A Grooming Routine

As a man who takes an interest in his appearance, you probably wash and shave every morning before dressing. You may not yet be using a 'refreshing' or 'moisturizing' product, but the addition of these two extra steps (with the correct products) into your daily routine takes no time at all and will keep your skin in peak condition. Remember, also, that smooth, young, good-looking skin on a man has close-up benefits that your partner will appreciate too.

A simple yet complete skincare routine doesn't require hours in the bathroom – just a few extra minutes each day. When you see and feel the results you will agree that the effort is well worth it. It can be hard to break a habit or routine, so a gradual introduction on a product-by-product basis may be easier if you are currently just using soap, water and a razor.

Above: A regular grooming routine does not have to mean spending hours in the bathroom.

Four-Step System

1. CLEANSE ➧ 2. SHAVE ➧ 3. REFRESH ➧ 4. MOISTURIZE

The first step every morning is to cleanse your face to remove dirt and other impurities and to prepare and soften the skin for shaving. The next step is to shave – a wet shave is kinder to the skin on a regular basis than electric razors, which are best used only intermittently. After shaving, a 'regulating' lotion should be used to help cool and refresh the face. Finally, the moisturizing step ensures that the skin is adequately hydrated and protected against the detrimental effects of the environment described earlier.

Ideally, this routine should be repeated at night, if possible (omitting the shaving step, of course). Don't forget to pack a wash gel, refreshing lotion and moisturizer in you gym bag too, as sweating and showering always result in moisture loss.

1. Cleanse

Men's skin has larger pores than women's, so they become more easily clogged by oil (sebum) and dirt. Excess sebum production also attracts bacteria, which can lead to outbreaks of spots. The cleanser you use needs, therefore, to be strong enough to remove pore-clogging oil and dirt, yet gentle enough to be used every day. Many bars of soap have a high pH level which is too acidic and therefore drying for the skin. It is better to select a foaming gel product which is designed for use on the face with a pH level compatible with the skin's natural pH (pH is a measure of acidity, which in human skin is about 5.5).

2. Shave

Again, a normal bar of soap does not contain the right properties for a close comfortable shave. A very rich lather is required to help the razor glide over the surface of the skin cells without doing too much damage to the cells but managing to cut the hairs at the same time. A mousse formulation gives the best consistency and can also be very cost-effective – up to sixty shaves should be expected from each can. Formulations enriched with conditioners will leave your skin feeling exceptionally smooth afterwards.

3. Refresh

After shaving, saturate a cotton wool pad with a refreshing lotion and smooth it gently over your face with outward movements – never drag the skin downwards. Used daily, this will rid the skin of any remaining excess surface oil as well as traces of shaving cream/mousse. Make sure such a lotion does not contain alcohol as this will have a drying effect on the skin, and *never* use a perfumed aftershave lotion on your face – if you want to smell nice, use eau de toilette or cologne behind your neck or on your wrists. Refreshing lotion should leave your face feeling cool, but definitely not stinging and itchy.

Left: Always take your grooming products to the gym - your hair and skin need treatment after exercising.

4. Moisturize

Although a man's skin is naturally oilier than a woman's it is still at risk from the drying effects of environment and lifestyle – the sun, central heating, alcohol, smoking and so on. Dryness causes the skin to lose its resilience and elasticity and eventually leads to the unwelcome appearance of lines and wrinkles. The most noticeable lines on a man's face appear first at the sides of the eyes, nose and mouth, which all point downwards to give a generally 'sagging' look to the face – women also get lines on the eyelids, forehead and top lip, so be thankful!

With men's skin, however, it is important not to confuse oiliness with the amount of moisture in the skin. A man's skin may be oily on the surface but still lack moisture underneath. This situation requires a light, non-greasy moisturizer which can be absorbed quickly to deliver moisture where it is needed without leaving a sticky 'after-feel' on the skin's surface. Many women's moisturizers (particularly night creams) are too heavy for a man's more oily skin and will simply sit on the surface and not reach the lower layers. Don't forget to apply moisturizer to your throat too – particularly if your beard/shaving zone extends to that area and you are constantly removing the top layer of skin.

Decoding the Jargon

Due to the proliferation of female skin care products and advice over past decades, women are quite familiar with the terminology and claims of packaging and advertisements. In case you don't know your AHAs from your SPFs, here is a quick guide to the most commonly used terminology on skincare products.

Hypo-Allergenic

This means the product has been rigorously tested to minimize the risk of allergenic reactions or skin irritation. No product can claim to be totally free from ingredients which can cause allergic reactions but this term means that the most common irritants – alcohol, lanolin, perfume and so on – have been omitted. The package will sometimes simply state 'Dermatologically Tested'.

Non-Comedogenic

This means that the product has been designed with ingredients which will not clog the pores (comedone is the technical term for a blackhead). This claim is usually made of products which are left on the skin – refreshing lotion say, or moisturizer – but not of washing products, which after use are removed from the skin with water.

Glycolipids

These are special skin conditioning ingredients which help hydrate the skin by retarding moisture in the upper cell layers, causing them to plump up. The result is smoother-looking skin with less visible lines and wrinkles. (Wrinkles cannot be 'eliminated' or 'removed' – just made 'less visible'.)

AHAs

The term Alpha Hydroxy Acids may sound scary, but all it actually means is naturally occurring fruit acids. It has been discovered that daily use of AHAs speeds up the skin's natural exfoliation process, resulting in improved texture and overall appearance. The gentle sloughing action of such creams is better for men than the use of facial scrubs (creams containing abrasive particles to remove dead skin cells) because of the amount of abrasion a man's skin already suffers from the action of the razor.

SPFs

Sun Protection Factors are numbers which help you estimate how long you can withstand sun exposure before burning while wearing that particular product. Many facial moisturizers now contain an SPF to protect the skin from the harmful effects of the sun even in the winter. A moisturizer containing an SPF is not, however, sufficient protection for holiday sunbathing, when a reputable suncare product – an oil, cream or lotion – should also be used for maximum protection.

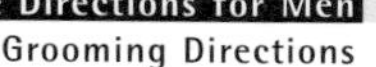

Holiday Sun Protection

The current rapid increase in the numbers of people contracting skin cancer from over-exposure to the sun is causing great concern. Research has shown that far fewer men than women bother to wear a sun protection product, in the mistaken belief that male skin is less prone to sun damage. All men, especially fair-skinned ones, need an assortment of sun creams and after-sun preparations for time spent in hot climates, as it can take only one bad case of sunburn to result in skin cancer many years later. It is important to know your personal tanning type, and then buy the correct products for the amount of time you expect to be in the sun each day, (see the information on SPFs below).

- **Type 1:** Fair or red hair, pale skin (often freckled). Maximum time you can stay unprotected without burning: 10 minutes. **Suggested SPF: 15 and above.**
- **Type 2:** Fair/mousey hair, pale eyes, fair to medium skin. Maximum time you can stay unprotected without burning: 10–15 minutes. **Suggested SPF 10–15.**
- **Type 3:** Dark hair and eyes, fair to medium skin. Maximum time you can stay unprotected without burning: 15–20 minutes. **Suggested SPF: 8 and above.**
- **Type 4:** Dark hair and eyes, olive to dark skin. Maximum time you can stay unprotected without burning: 20 minutes or more, depending how dark your natural skin colour is. **Suggested SPF: 6–8**.

When you know your type, do a simple sum to find out how long an SPF cream will allow you to sunbathe. If your skin type allows 10 minutes of exposure without protection, a cream with SPF15 gives you 15 x 10 minutes = 150 minutes (or two and a half hours) before you begin to burn.
Remember to reapply your sunscreen after swimming (even if the product claims to be waterproof) and invest in a good 'aftersun' cream/lotion to cool and moisturize your skin after sun exposure.

Left: Remember also to use SPF products for outdoor sporting activities, and not just on the beach.

Looking after Your Hair

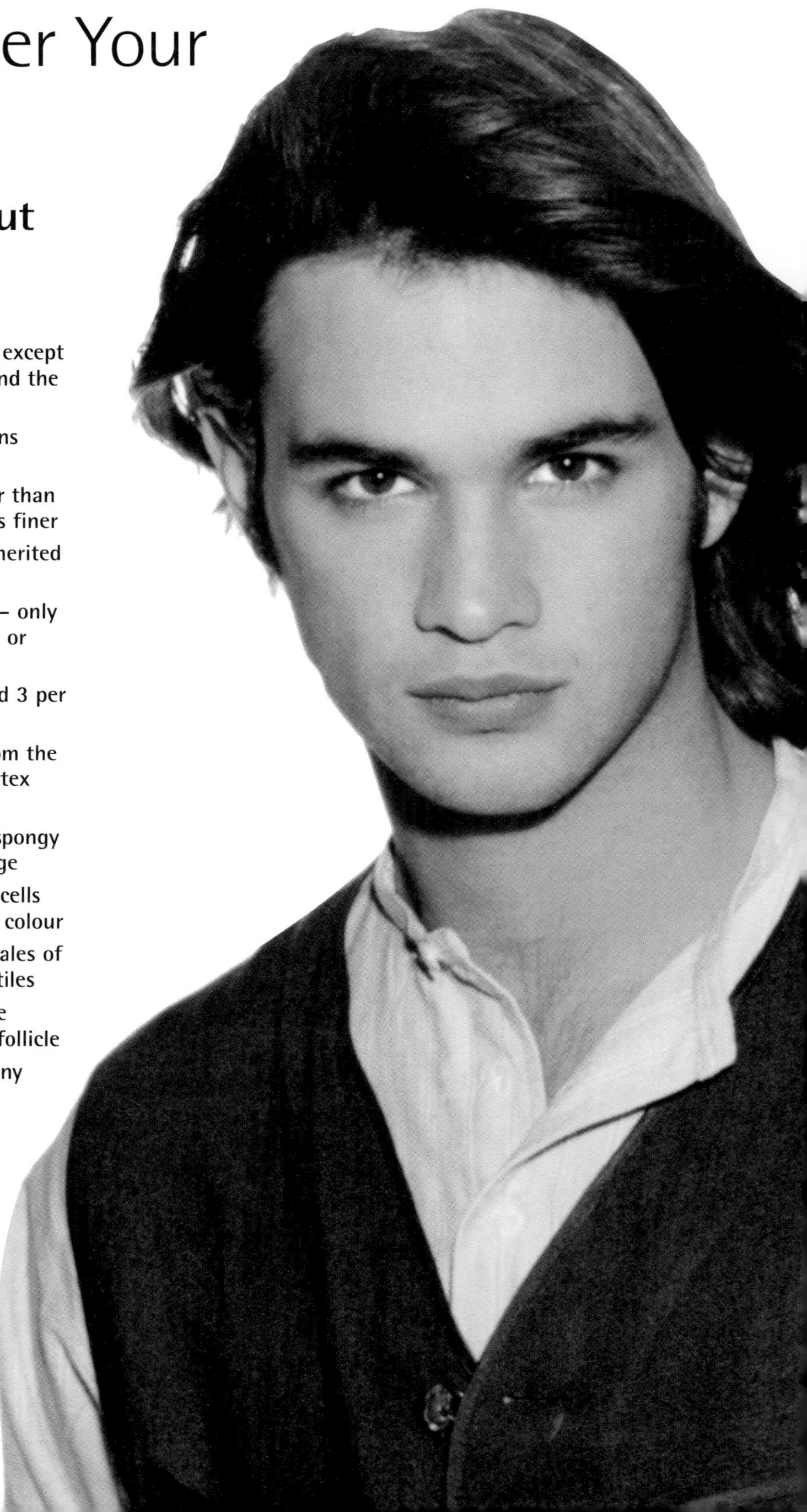

Fifteen Facts about Hair

- Hair grows all over your body except on the palms of your hands and the soles of your feet
- An average adult scalp contains approximately 100,000 hairs
- Blonds tend to have more hair than brunettes or redheads but it is finer
- Texture and curliness is an inherited feature
- The hair itself is dead matter – only the root, deep within the hole or hair follicle, is alive
- Hair is 97 per cent protein and 3 per cent moisture
- Each hair has three layers (from the inside outwards): medulla, cortex and cuticle
- The medulla consists of soft, spongy cells which deteriorate with age
- The cortex consists of fibrous cells which contain the pigment or colour
- The cuticle consists of hard scales of keratin that overlap like roof tiles
- Oil (sebum) is produced by the sebaceous gland in each hair follicle
- Lubrication is stimulated by tiny muscles around the follicle
- These tiny muscles are what make your hair 'stand on end' when you are afraid
- A single hair 'grows' for between two and six years
- Grey hair does not exist – it is an illusion caused by white hairs (which contain no pigment at all) mixed with darker hairs

Which Products?

Because hair is essentially 'dead matter' it is very easy for it to look limp, lank or simply unhealthy unless it is looked after properly with the right products. In past centuries this was extremely difficult because people had only harsh soaps and cold water – in certain periods men preferred to wear wigs than to have their own shabby hair on display! Today, thankfully, every man can have healthy, attractive hair due to products which combine modern technology with natural ingredients. Most product ranges divide into three categories for the most common haircare problems: dry hair, oily hair and scalp problems (dandruff).

Left: Long hair in particular should always look well-groomed, healthy and shiny. If you are short of time, tie it back in a plain, dark band.

Dry hair

Hair normally becomes drier with age, although dryness can also be caused by excessive use of a hairdryer and by exposure to sunlight or harsh chemicals such as chlorine or bleach. Dry hair appears dull and stiff and, unless it is trimmed regularly, will break short and suffer from split ends. This hair type needs products which will replenish lost moisture and add shine, though only a good haircut will get rid of split ends or badly damaged hair. However, a moisturizing shampoo and deep moisturizing conditioner containing ingredients such as almond oil and wheat protein will help to replenish moisture and add shine by assisting the cuticle layers to lie flat again. If your hair is prone to dryness, also look for shampoos and conditioners containing a sunscreen (especially when you are going on holiday) to help prevent further damage. Long hair may be very dry at the ends because the natural sebum does not reach that far – in such instances, leave the conditioner on your hair for several minutes before rinsing.

Oily hair

Over-production of sebum at the base of the hair shaft results in oily or greasy hair which tends to lie flat and limp close to the head and is difficult to style successfully.

This hair type needs a deep cleansing shampoo and only a light conditioner. Ingredients such as rosemary or nettles are effective for removing grease but gentle enough to use frequently. Men with oily hair often use too much shampoo in an attempt to remove the grease – it's better to cut down the amount you use and concentrate on massaging the scalp, which is where the oil is produced. Good rinsing is essential and should always be done with clean, warm water. Don't use the bath water as a final rinse because the body's skin cells and dirt will attach themselves to your hair! The water should not be too hot, as higher temperatures stimulate oil production. Use only a light conditioner, and don't leave it on your hair for too long before rinsing off.

Problem scalp (dandruff)

Dandruff is caused when the cells on the scalp develop too rapidly into their hard, keratinized form. When there are too many of them to be removed by normal shampooing and combing, they stick together and fall off in flakes – leaving the tell-tale signs on your shoulders. Anti-dandruff shampoos and conditioners help to deal with this problem by the use of an active ingredient called zinc pyrithione. If your dandruff problem does not respond to zinc pyrithione, a coal-tar product may be more effective – some people find that alternating between the two ingredients is the most effective method of control. If neither ingredient solves your dandruff problem, consult your doctor as you may have another, less common medical condition which needs different treatment. If you do have dandruff, it is essential to clean your combs and brushes regularly after use.

Hair in a hurry

If you don't have time for shampoos and conditioners, there are now many two-in-one products on the market which claim to clean and condition your hair with one swift application. This may be great for business trips, holidays or sports changing rooms, but remember that such products are for convenience only, and prolonged use is not good for your hair. All two-in-ones leave a conditioning residue which cannot be washed

Above: City slicker – hair gel not only gives control but can add extra style points to either long or short hair.

away by the same product. A build-up results, which attracts dirt and pollution and therefore makes hair more dirty more quickly – which requires more product. Quite a vicious circle! If you have found yourself in this situation, only a separate shampoo (one without a built-in conditioner) will remove the residue.

Successful styling

Today there is a huge range of products to make styling your hair much easier. If you want to achieve volume, lift or control in certain areas, there will be a spray, gel, mousse or wax to help you do it. Again this is nothing new – men used waxes, oils, creams and pomades for centuries – but new technologies have produced modern products which are non-sticky, easy to wash out and smell good too!

Most styling products can be used on either damp or dry hair, as a styling aid or as a 'finishing' product. It is generally best to towel-dry the hair first before applying any product, as this will make styling easier and the products more effective. To give your hair more fullness and volume, use a gel or mousse at the roots and lift the hair at right-angles from the scalp with a brush or your fingers when drying the hair. Whenever you use a dryer on your hair, use a styling product to help protect your hair from the heat.

Mousse is good for fine or thin hair and will give moderate hold. Gel gives a firmer hold and is good for dry, thick or curly hair which is difficult to control. Gel can also be used to slick back hair either for the beach (look for one containing sunscreen) or for a night on the town (especially if you haven't had time to wash your hair!). When applying mousse or gel, apply it to your hand first, not directly on to the hair, to prevent stickiness and uneven application.

Chapter 6

Wardrobe Directions

Now that we have finished the analysis of your face, body, proportions, colouring and so on, we need to conduct a much simpler examination – the contents of your wardrobe. All the information you have gleaned about your physical characteristics can finally be put into practice and you can start to plan a flexible, versatile wardrobe. From the previous chapters you probably already have a few ideas about items that you would like to buy, but before you do it's useful to assess your existing clothes and clear a little space for the new additions.

Above: Take a leaf out of the women's book – get your wardrobe organised to keep your clothes in tip-top condition.

Closet Encounters

The chances are that weeding out your clothes is a job that never crosses your mind! It really is worthwhile, however, as it helps you to see where you have too many of certain types of clothes and where you have gaps. So heap all your clothes on to the bed and start to seperate them into three piles:

Pile No. 1: Clothes Worn Frequently

These can go back into the wardrobe as you probably like and feel comfortable in all these garments – it is likely that they suit your shape, colouring, proportions and so forth. Also, they will tend to be quite recent purchases and therefore current in style, cut and fabric.

Pile No. 2: Clothes Worn Sometimes

These probably consist of 'occasional' wear (holidays, formal wear and so on) or items which don't quite fit into your lifestyle. These can go back too, but you must think of different ways of wearing them in order to incorporate them more fully into your wardrobe. You may need to buy some extra garments to combine with them for versatility.

Pile No. 3: Clothes Not Worn for Several Years

You have to be ruthless and get rid of these clothes! Research shows that if you have not worn certain items for two or three years, the chances are that you will never wear them again. Think of the reasons why you don't wear them – they probably don't fit you; are old-fashioned; are wrong for your shape or colouring; are unwanted Christmas or birthday presents (probably from your mother!); or belong to a life you used to lead but don't now.

Be realistic: you are probably not going to lose enough weight to squeeze back into them; if they come back into fashion again you'll be so much older that you'll look ridiculous in them; your mother has probably forgotten she ever gave you a stripy tank-top; and it is pointless to hang on to cut-off jeans from when you were a student. It is best to bag up the whole lot and take them to a charity shop. If some of the items are relatively expensive and in good condition (suits, jackets and coats, for instance) 'nearly new' shops will buy them from you and this extra cash can be put towards some new purchases.

Organizing Your Wardrobe

While we're being ruthless, don't forget to extend the weeding session to your socks, underwear, ties, belts, shoes and so on. As with the clothes, get rid of anything which is never worn or is generally tatty or ancient. Now you can begin to organize the surviving, wearable garments in ways which are space-saving and protective, as well as making items easy to view when you are in a rush to get dressed in the morning.

It is worthwhile investing in the following:

- Large plastic or wooden coathangers with wide 'arms' to keep the shoulder-shape in jackets (get rid of all wire hangers).
- Wooden 'roll-bar' hangers for trousers to prevent across-the-knee creases which thin hangers always produce. The more expensive types have rubber strips across the bar to prevent trousers sliding off.
- Tie organizers to fix inside your wardrobe door so that ties can be hung straight to let creases fall out after each wearing.
- Belt organizers to be hung from your wardrobe rail – never roll up belts in a drawer as this can cause the leather to crack. Alternatively, belts can be hung from the metal hook of your coathangers.
- Drawer organizers: bendy pieces of plastic which form

neat compartments for small rolled up items such as socks, underwear and handkerchiefs.

- Shoe organizers to keep shoes tidy and in pairs. Leather shoes and boots are best stored on wire or wooden racks at the base of the wardrobe; casual shoes such as pumps/espadrilles can be slotted into canvas organizers which can be hung from a rail or on the inside of the wardrobe door.
- Shirt/sweater organizers: inexpensive canvas shelves which can be suspended inside your wardrobe. These are extremely useful if you are short of drawer space or find it difficult to retrieve folded items from deep drawers. Similar but more expensive storage facilities are also available as a series of stacking wire trays which can be kept inside or outside your actual wardrobe.

Clothes Maintenance

The effort involved in having the right clothes for your shape, colouring, lifestyle and so on will be wasted if you don't look after them properly to keep them looking as good as yourself. Not only that, but your clothes and accessories will last longer if they are cleaned correctly and on a regular basis. It goes without saying that clothing worn directly next to the skin such as shirts, socks and underwear should be washed after one wearing; garments which are worn over others, such as sweaters, jackets and trousers, should be left unworn between wearings for several days to let the air circulate between the fibres. It is a good idea to hang clothes outside a wardrobe at least overnight, until cool and dry. Shoes should also be left for a couple of days between wearings to let the leather 'breathe' and allow any bad odours to escape! It is a good idea to clean your shoes when you take them off, as the polish will sink easily into the warm leather and help condition the shoes overnight.

Top right: Canvas hanging shelves provide easy-to-view storage for sweaters, T-shirts and undies.
Right: Shoes can be stored on stylish wooden racks or, if your short of floorspace, in a hanging bag on the back of the door.
Far right: Invest in tie-racks, belt hangers and perhaps even a wooden valet stand to keep your clothes crease-free overnight.

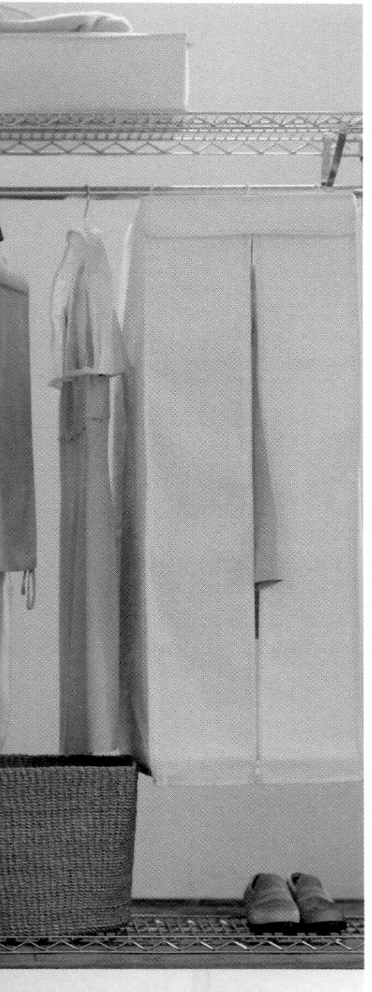

Cleaning

Always look at the washing/cleaning instructions on a garment before you decide to buy it. Do you have the time/patience/ expertise to hand-wash a sweater? If not, look for one with a 'machine-wash' label. Many garments now have labels advising 'dry-clean only' – this may be fine for your suits, jackets and formal trousers, but think carefully about the bills you will run up on more casual items. Excessive or badly executed dry-cleaning can also shorten the life of a garment because of the harsh chemicals involved. Also, never leave cleaned garments inside the plastic wrapper as this traps the fumes inside. Always remove the bag (throw out the wire hanger) and leave the garment to hang in a well-ventilated room overnight to remove the chemical odours. Find a specialist cleaner for suede or leather items – these may be more expensive than standard high street cleaners, but the result will be worth it.

Stains

Never attempt to remove a stain from a dry-clean-only garment (especially a silk tie) with soap and water. Water can sometimes 'set' the stain and make it far more difficult to remove, even by dry-cleaning. Dry-clean aerosol sprays and silk-tie-protector sprays can be purchased to deal with inevitable small stains, but if you have any doubts at all seek professional help rather than ruin your garment. Stains on suede shoes can be removed effectively with an aerosol suede shampoo and a soft plastic brush – a nail brush or plastic washing-up brush is far better than a wire brush (often recommended for suede), which can damage the soft finish. Stains on washable garments can be treated by applying stain-removal sprays or blocks directly on to the stained area before following the normal washing instructions.

Ironing

For all the men in the world who have never been taught how to iron a shirt, here is the idiot's guide to the task which women hate the most.

Learn how to do this, and women will love you forever !

Idiot's Guide to Ironing a Shirt

Preparation

Lightly dampen your shirts all over with a water spray and leave loosely rolled for at least half an hour.

Collar

It is best to start with the collar. Remove any collar stiffeners (I recommend removing them before washing). Beginning with the underside of the collar and neckband, iron from the outside edge to the centre, then repeat for the opposite side. This avoids creases forming at the points and helps to eliminate any expansion caused by dampening as cotton fibres naturally relax when wet. While it is still damp and warm turn the collar over, holding each collar point between your thumb and forefinger, pull taut to straighten the front edge and stretch the outside edge.

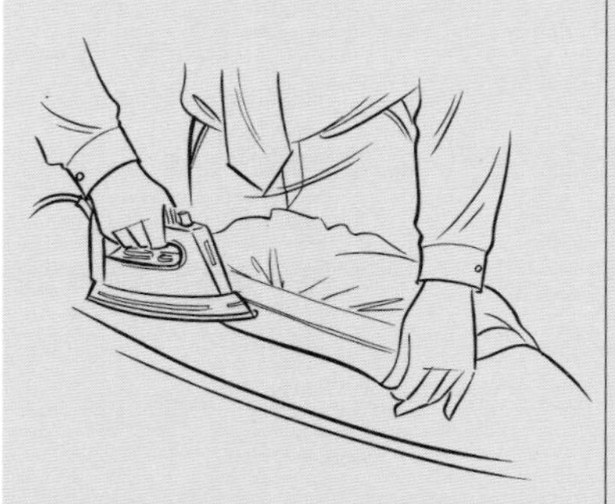

This helps prevent the collar points curling under when worn. Repeat the previous ironing process on the right side. If you prefer a crisper-looking collar, spray a little starch on the right side before ironing. Finally, fold the collar along the neckband seam and iron to create a definite fold.

Cuffs

Iron the cuffs before the body of the shirt as they have a natural stiffness and will not easily crease once ironed. Follow the same principle as for ironing the collar. Start with the underside, ironing from the outside edge to the centre. Repeat this process on the right side. With French (double) cuffs, fold the cuff in half, line up the cufflink holes and press a firm crease along the fold. Spray starch is optional for cuffs.

Sleeves

Place one sleeve at a time on the ironing board with the gauntlet (wrist) opening uppermost. Spread out the sleeve, aiming to avoid creases (watch out for folds underneath, as you will be ironing both sides at once). Use mist spray if necessary, then iron from the underarm seam towards the top edge of the sleeve, forming a crease along the top edge. Pull out the material at the cuff as you carefully push the point of the iron into the pleats and gathers. Turn the sleeve over and repeat.

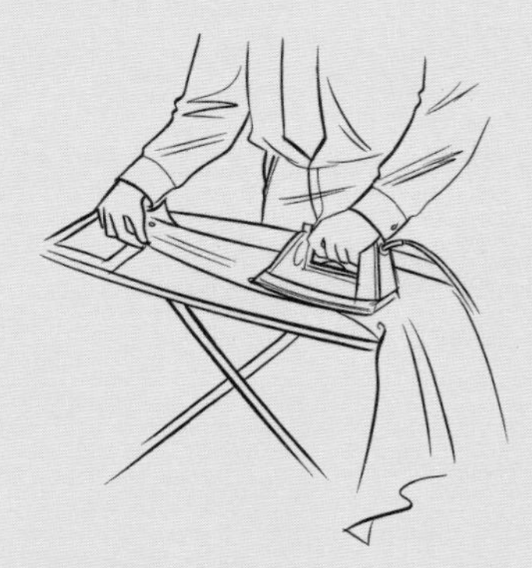

Yoke

It is best to iron one half of the yoke at a time. Lay one half over the end of the ironing board (with the toe of the board angled towards the sleeve). Spread out the fabric to eliminate any creases. With the point of the iron, work from the sleeve towards the centre join in the yoke. Swing the shirt around and repeat for the other half of the yoke.

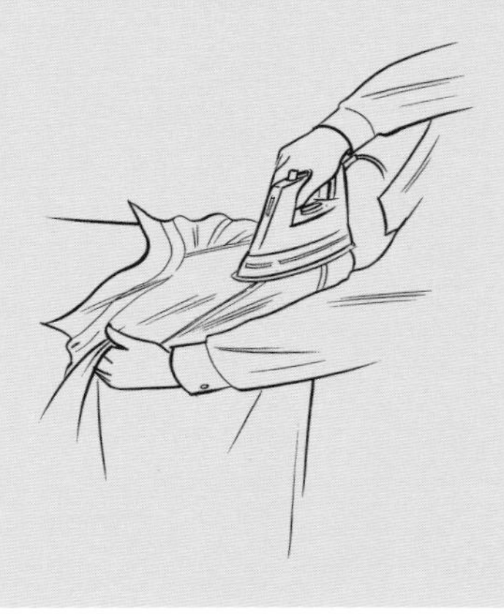

Back

Lay the back of the shirt body over the ironing board with the collar at the narrow end of the board. Iron from the tail to the yoke, mist spraying with water if necessary, but be careful to avoid spraying areas already ironed. Move the back across the board and finish off the rest of the back. Use the point of the iron around the armhole seams. Note: Creases easily return when the fabric is warm and damp, so when ironing large areas such as backs and fronts, make sure each section is as cool and dry as possible before moving on to the next.

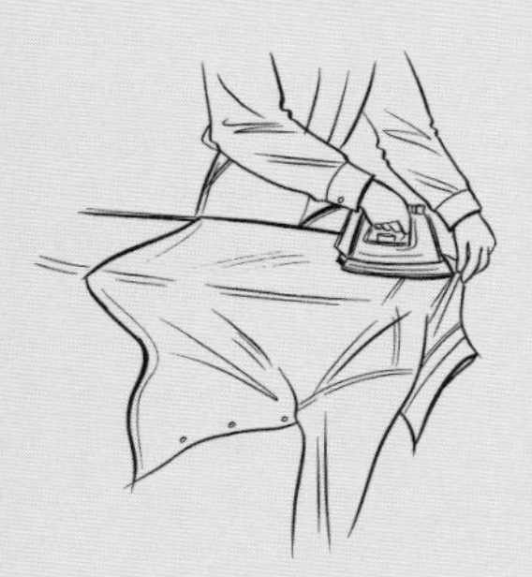

Front

Pull the shirt diagonally across the ironing board so that the end of the board is in the top of the armhole. Iron around the seam. Move the shirt front around the board so you have covered every area, using the point of the iron to get between the buttons.

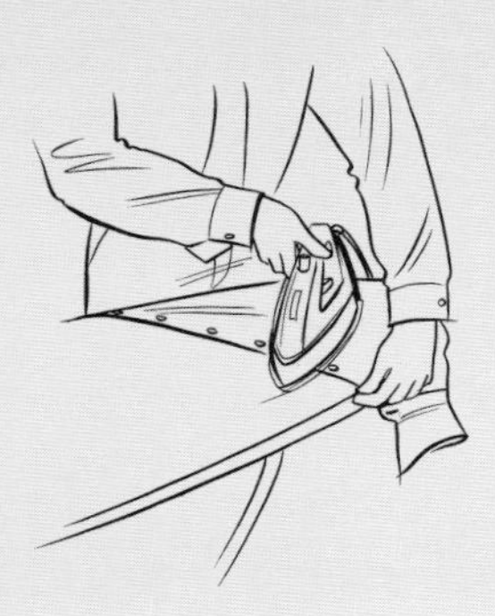

Repeat on the other side. Run the iron along the buttonhole front from the tail up to the collar, pulling lightly to stretch the material.

Airing

Fasten the top button and place on a plastic coathanger to air for at least thirty minutes in an open room before placing in your wardrobe or folding to put in a drawer.

Folding

Button up the shirt and place face down on a flat surface. Take a standard glossy magazine and place it at the centre of the yoke right up to the edge of the shoulder. Fold the side nearest to you over the magazine, lay the sleeve parallel with the folded edge, then fold the sleeve with three or four folds, concertina fashion, to fit within the dimensions of the magazine.

Fold the opposite side and sleeve in a similar manner. Make a fold at the shirt tail, then bring the fold up to the shoulders, wrapping as tightly as possible around the magazine. Turn the folded shirt over, remove the magazine and stack the shirts top to tail.

Removing creases

If shirts have been folded for a long time or subjected to a lot of pressure in a suitcase, the creases can easily be removed by hanging the shirts over a hot, steamy bath – a useful tip for men who travel frequently.

Warning

Some older steam irons can seriously damage your shirt! Check that your iron has smooth edges around the steam holes. Older models with sharp edges will wear collars and cuffs, reducing a shirt's life by up to 50 per cent.

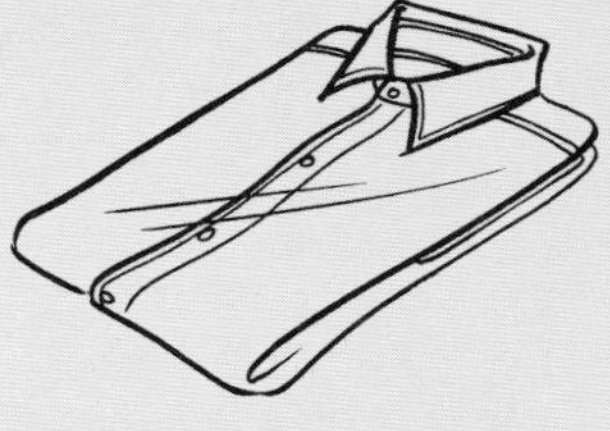

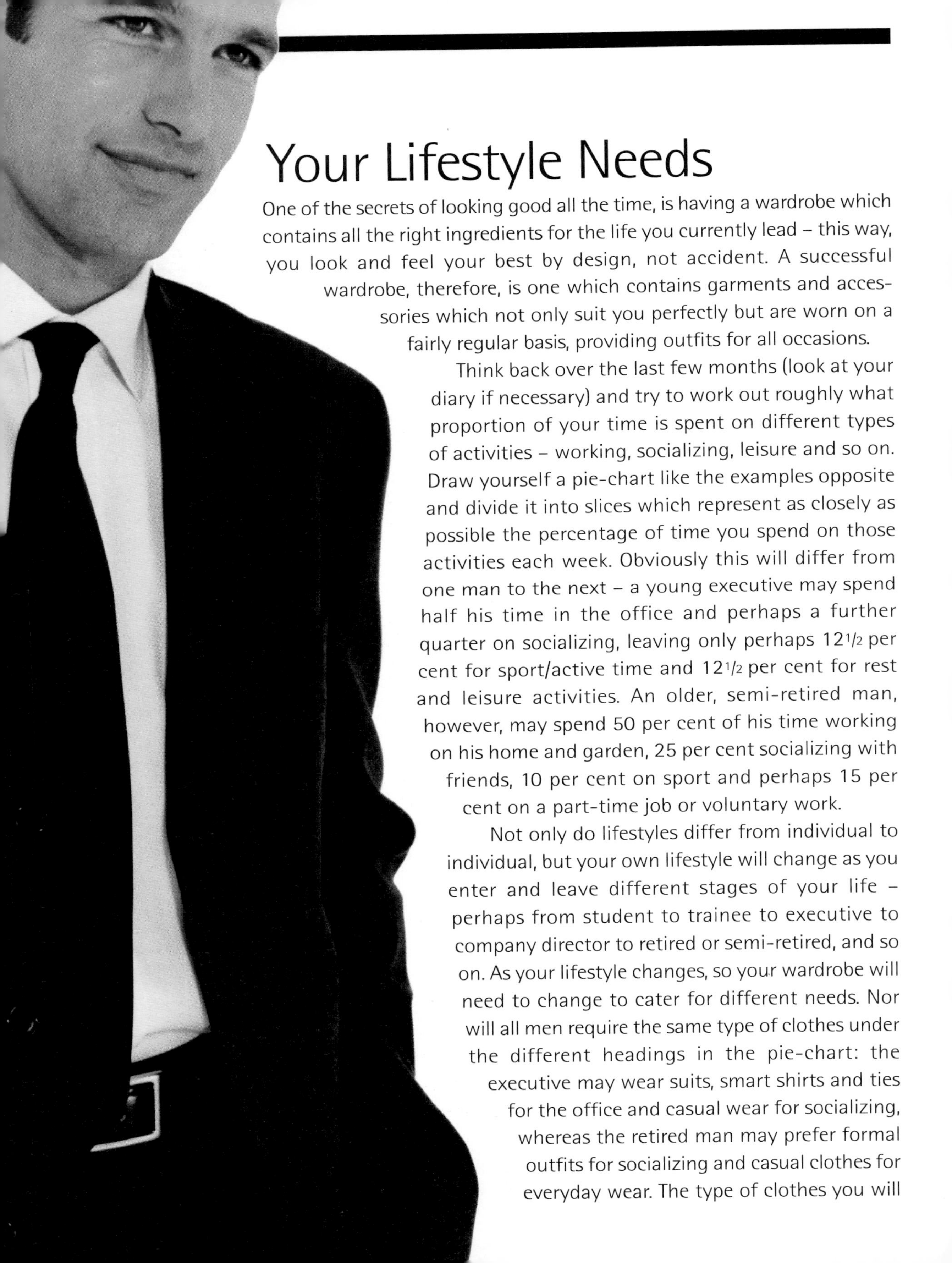

Your Lifestyle Needs

One of the secrets of looking good all the time, is having a wardrobe which contains all the right ingredients for the life you currently lead – this way, you look and feel your best by design, not accident. A successful wardrobe, therefore, is one which contains garments and accessories which not only suit you perfectly but are worn on a fairly regular basis, providing outfits for all occasions.

Think back over the last few months (look at your diary if necessary) and try to work out roughly what proportion of your time is spent on different types of activities – working, socializing, leisure and so on. Draw yourself a pie-chart like the examples opposite and divide it into slices which represent as closely as possible the percentage of time you spend on those activities each week. Obviously this will differ from one man to the next – a young executive may spend half his time in the office and perhaps a further quarter on socializing, leaving only perhaps 12½ per cent for sport/active time and 12½ per cent for rest and leisure activities. An older, semi-retired man, however, may spend 50 per cent of his time working on his home and garden, 25 per cent socializing with friends, 10 per cent on sport and perhaps 15 per cent on a part-time job or voluntary work.

Not only do lifestyles differ from individual to individual, but your own lifestyle will change as you enter and leave different stages of your life – perhaps from student to trainee to executive to company director to retired or semi-retired, and so on. As your lifestyle changes, so your wardrobe will need to change to cater for different needs. Nor will all men require the same type of clothes under the different headings in the pie-chart: the executive may wear suits, smart shirts and ties for the office and casual wear for socializing, whereas the retired man may prefer formal outfits for socializing and casual clothes for everyday wear. The type of clothes you will

Working executive lifestyle

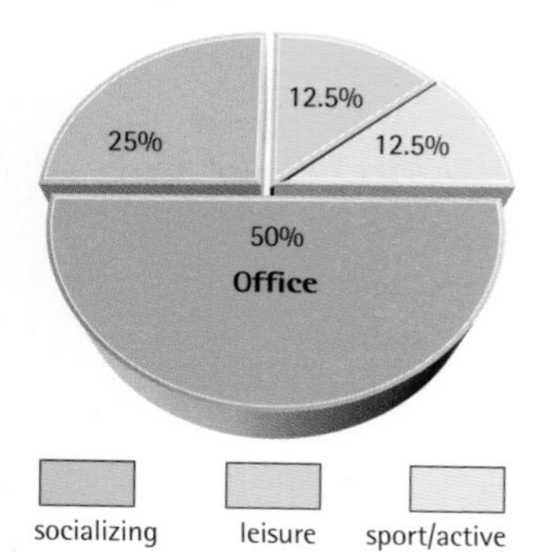

Retired/self-employed lifestyle

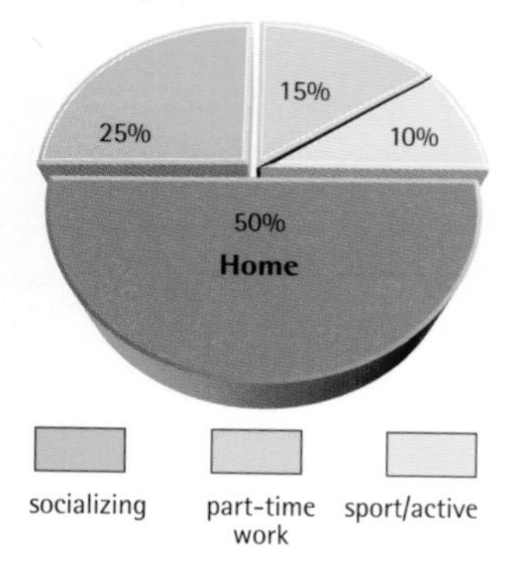

Work **(left)** or play **(right)**, analyze your lifestyle to balance your wardrobe requirements.

need for your wardrobe are therefore dependent not just on your lifestyle but also on your own tastes, preferences and personality.

Investment Buying

Once you have completed your pie-chart, you should have a rough idea of the percentage of clothes you need within each category. If, for example, most of your waking time is spent at work but you have far more leisure/weekend/casual clothes than workwear, you know where your money should be spent. One young man whose insurance company sent him for a consultation possessed only one suit which he had worn every day for two years – the trousers were so thin that you could see his underpants through the fabric! The rest of his wardrobe consisted of thousands of pounds, worth of designer casual

wear which was, if at all, only worn at weekends.

You need to look and feel good for the majority of the time, not just when you 'go out' – particularly if you are looking to advance speedily in your career. This means spending most money on the clothes you wear most often and working out a monthly budget for these important purchases. Most men will budget for outgoings such as housing, socializing, holidays and car, but few consider doing so for clothing. Look at your monthly income and your existing monthly outgoings, and work out what percentage you would be able to put aside for your future wardrobe needs. Then stick to it – just as you do for the car and the mortgage!

Plugging the Holes

With your pie-chart highlighting your 'needy' wardrobe zones and with a little space now cleared to incorporate some new buys, it is time to look in more detail at the different options for garments to plug the holes in your wardrobe. Listed below are the items which will provide outfits to cover all occasions. Column 1 contains garments for a smart or formal look. Column 2 contains garments for a less formal or semi-casual look. Column 3 contains garments for a totally casual look. In today's fashion world, however, formal and casual garments can also be

Smart	Semi-casual	Casual
☐ Suits	☐ Blazer	☐ Casual shirts
☐ Formal shirts	☐ Sports jacket	☐ T-shirts
☐ Ties	☐ Slacks/chinos	☐ Chunky knits
☐ Dinner jacket	☐ Polo-shirts	☐ Jeans/cargo pants
☐ Topcoat	☐ Fine knits	☐ Casual jacket

Above: Your wardrobe needs a selection of smart, semi-casual and casual items to cover all aspects of your lifestyle.

combined (for instance a formal suit with a T-shirt or polo-neck sweater) to give an even greater range of outfits and provide plenty of opportunities to develop a more personal style rather than the standard 'uniform' look.

You don't need to possess all the items listed opposite, because, as mentioned earlier, your lifestyle may not require all these areas to be covered. Also, your particular body shape or proportions may mean that certain garments don't suit you, or perhaps some are not right for your personality and self-image. No matter what your shape, size or lifestyle, however, aim to tick at least ten of the fifteen categories opposite for a comprehensive and versatile wardrobe. Then study the descriptions in Chapter 7 to help select your best fashion options within each category.

Chapter 7

Fashion Directions

Within each category of men's clothing there are a range of different options to choose from – some very traditional and classic, others more contemporary or current. Remember also that by combining unusual or conflicting items a high-fashion or trendy look can be achieved if that is what you prefer. Don't think that you have to adopt a similar look all the time – although you may need a classic look at work, you can experiment with a more contemporary or even trendy look for your leisure or socializing time.

Above: Suits in fashionable fabrics, cuts or colours will have a more limited life in your wardrobe than classic varieties.

Suits

Navy Blue

A plain blue suit is the most versatile and internationally accepted suit and therefore the 'safest' choice for most men. Navy suits all Colour Directions and can be teamed with a wide variety of shirt and tie colours and accessories. If you require only one suit for your wardrobe, this is your best choice. Navy suits can also be split much more easily than other colours to wear with different garments, for instance a navy suit jacket, jeans and a white T-shirt gives a relaxed, semi-casual look.

Grey

This is the colour most associated with the world of business and can be seen as faceless or staid (the 'men-in-grey-suits' syndrome) unless combined with a contemporary tie and accessories. Men with a Warm Colour Direction must take care not to look 'drained' or in need of a blood transfusion, and look best if the grey is teamed with a warm shirt and tie colour. Men with a Cool Colour Direction must also be careful not to fade away by being totally grey from head to toe – a crisp white shirt and bright tie are needed to relieve the boredom of an overall monotone look. Grey suits are more difficult to split than navy, but always look good teamed with black.

Birdseye

Sometimes known as nailhead, this is a fabric which mixes white fibres with grey to give a subtle dotted effect. It has slightly more depth and interest than a plain grey fabric and

Above: Suiting fabrics: plain, birdseye, chalk-stripe, pin-stripe, check

can be a particularly good alternative to a simple grey suit for men with Cool or Light colouring. As grey is the predominant background colour, birdseye also looks good teamed with black.

Striped

Pin-stripe or chalk-stripe suits have come to be regarded as the traditional attire of city businessmen and, together with the bowler hat and umbrella, were upheld in the past as the ultimate symbols of the British male! The pinstripes (fine stripes close together) and chalk-stripes (softer stripes further apart) can be woven into grey or navy fabric and are thought to derive from the parallel lines in ledgers – hence the connection with financial business. Stripes always make a short man look taller, provided the jacket is single- rather than double-breasted. Although striped suiting has long been associated with a conservative look, fashion designers are increasingly using the fabric in contemporary ways, for instance made up into a Nehru style to be worn with a casual shirt or sweater. Pin-stripe trousers look good on their own as a casual item with a white T-shirt and a pin-stripe waistcoat can look great with jeans. Avoid striped shirts with striped suits – a plain shirt with a modern tie gives an updated look.

Prince of Wales Check

This weave took its name from the Duke of Windsor, who was a big fan of loud patterns! Technically speaking, it is actually a black and white plaid with a thin blue overcheck and, although it took many years to become acceptable for formal occasions, it is today regarded as quite classic suiting. Compared to plain and pin-stripe fabrics, checks still have a sharper or more racy image and should definitely be avoided by men who are short or overweight as the strong horizontal lines add weight and width. Checks are notoriously difficult to combine with other patterns,

so be very careful with your choice of shirt and tie – a plain shirt and subtle tie look best.

Modern Suits

Young men are increasingly moving away from the traditional navy, grey, striped or check suits in favour of modern variations which differ in colour, fabric or cut. Colours such as olive green, brown, teal and aubergine are becoming quite acceptable in many businesses, particularly if they are cut in a traditional

Above: Suits can be so versatile: formal or informal; dressed up or down; traditional or modern – just suit yourself depending on your personality or the occasion.

style. Fabrics such as corduroy, linen or moleskin, however, always make a suit seem less formal and may therefore not be suitable for some business situations – they can, however, be ideal for semi-casual occasions, especially when worn with T-shirts, sweaters or polo-shirts. Remember that suits with a very modern cut or styling features will probably have a short and limited life in your wardrobe and do not constitute a good investment unless you have money to burn. An expensive suit should last for many years.

Above and right: Light coloured shirts give a classic or traditional look and are the easiest, safest option for most men. Deep coloured shirts give a more informal or fashionable look and need care in the selection of the colour for your particular Colour Direction. Note also that coloured cufflinks should always have a connection either to your shirt or tie colour.

Formal Shirts

Plain Shirts

These, in light colours, are the safest options for most men as they suit all Colour Directions and combine easily with most suit and tie patterns. Plain shirts in deep colours are more difficult as they need to suit your Colour Direction well (see Chapter 4) and often make the tie appear 'lighter', which can give an unwanted gangster-like image! Deep shirts with matching deep ties are a good fashionable alternative, especially for those with a Deep or Bright Colour Direction.

Striped Shirts

These are the second favourite option with most men, although their popularity within the fashion world tends to wax and wane. The general rule is that the narrower and lighter the stripe, the more conservative the shirt; the wider and bolder the stripe, the more racy or fashionable the shirt. Bold stripes made their biggest statement (together with loud ties and braces) in the financial capitals of the world during the boom years of the 1980s.

Check Shirts

These are the most difficult to wear successfully with suits. As with stripes, the smaller and finer the check, the more formal and conservative the shirt. As checks become larger, wearing a tie becomes harder – and when checks reach lumberjack proportions the shirt obviously becomes a casual item and a tie becomes totally unwearable.

Ties

Although this is the smallest garment a man wears, a tie can be incredibly important as it directs attention straight to the face and speaks volumes about a man's self-image, personality, status and so on. A tie serves no purpose whatsoever as an item of clothing, yet billions are sold around the world each year – such is their importance as a means of self-expression for men who must wear a suit every day to their place of work. Unlike women, men do not have the opportunity to express themselves

via a wide choice of hairstyles, jewellery or cosmetics, so a tie becomes their only piece of pure decoration. A good formal tie should be in a quality silk and lined with muslin to provide adequate bulk for a good knot. Thin polyester ties always cheapen a man's image.

Plain Ties

As with plain suits, plain ties are the easiest and safest option for any man. But remember to choose wisely for your Colour Direction, as the tie makes a direct connection to the face. Plain ties will not be boring if the quality is excellent and the colour

Above: The larger the check on a shirt the more difficult it becomes to wear a patterned tie. A plain tie is the best option.

perfect. For interest, look for two-tone silks which subtly change colour in different lights. Plain knit or nubbly ties in wool or silk can be good to give a more casual or semi-casual look, especially when worn with a check shirt or tweed jacket.

Striped Ties

Often viewed as quite conservative attire, these are associated with schools, colleges or regiments and, in the USA, with company representatives. The stripes can vary in width and are usually diagonal on a corded silk fabric. A new version of the striped tie, favoured by younger men today, sports horizontal stripes on a lightweight silk twill – a contemporary look for an old classic. When wearing a striped tie on a striped shirt, make sure the stripes are similar colours but of different scales or your onlookers will feel nauseous!

Patterned Ties

These give a man the widest choice of all, from classic foulards

(small geometric patterns woven into the fabric) to large abstract designs; from conservative pin dots to overscaled polka dots; from small paisleys and checks to huge florals and loud plaids. Unlike plain or striped ties, patterned ties are the ones which change most frequently with fashion. Keeping up with the latest trends in neckwear and accessories is one of the easiest ways to update your wardrobe and keep your look modern and in touch. Wearing a large, loud floral tie when the rest of the world is in subtle checks marks you as yesterday's man!

Formal Coats and Jackets

Dinner Jacket or Tuxedo

This is probably not a wardrobe must-have for the majority of men. If, however, you find yourself attending several black-tie functions per year and that situation looks likely to continue, it is probably worth investing in your own well-fitting DJ rather than hiring one of the (usually) ill-fitting varieties. Deep, Bright and Cool men look great in the stark contrast of black and white, but Light, Muted and Warm men may need to soften the effect with a bow tie and/or waistcoat in a more harmonious colour for their Colour Direction. However, a coloured shirt should never be worn with a DJ! Remember also that a cummerbund (especially a brightly coloured one) will draw attention to and expand a large waistline, while a thin elasticated bow-tie on a small wing collar will draw attention to a fat neck and/or double chin. A single-breasted waistcoat and a quality, tied-by-hand bow-tie with a turned-down collar are the most flattering choices for most men.

Angular and soft faces both suit a bow-tie in a plain fabric. For patterned bow-ties, follow the guidelines of your face when selecting the pattern. (Soft faces should avoid wing-collared shirts which can look too harsh – a turned-down collar is more flattering.)

Left: If you find yourself attending regular black-tie functions, it may be worth investing in your own dinner jacket, dress shirt and silk bow-tie.

Tying a Bow Tie

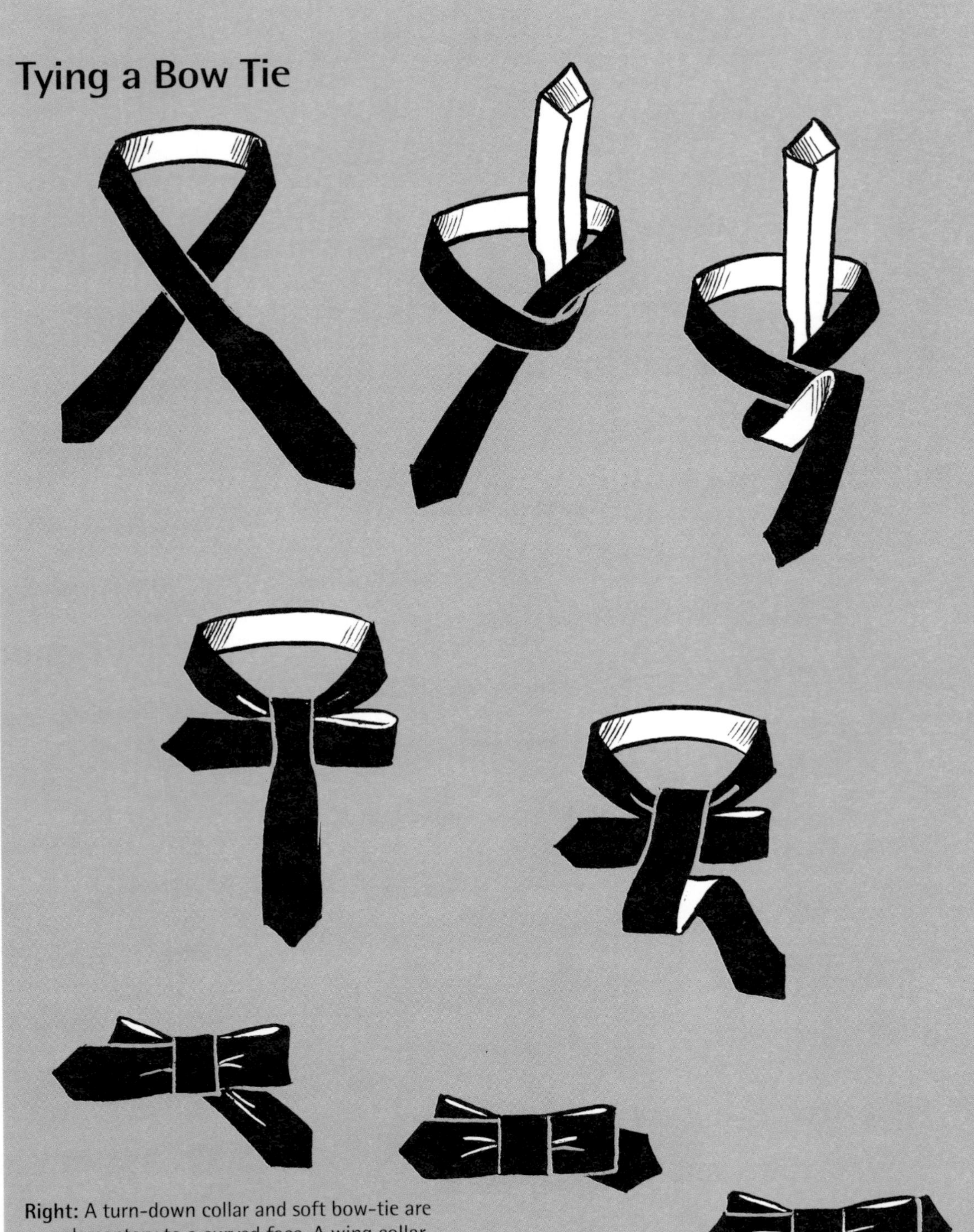

Right: A turn-down collar and soft bow-tie are complementary to a curved face. A wing collar and crisp bow tie are more flattering to an angular face.

Top Coat

A man who wears formal suits, shirts and ties (and even a DJ) on a regular basis, will need one or more topcoats for extra warmth and protection from the elements when travelling. A woollen overcoat is useful for those who live in or regularly visit colder climates, but those who live and work in warmer climates may prefer to have a more lightweight garment such as a trench coat. Some raincoats today have a versatile, detachable woollen lining, making them the ideal choice for men who need a topcoat for all seasons.

Always wear a suit when shopping for a topcoat, as the size needs to be big enough to accommodate several layers of garments beneath. Short or contoured men should avoid belted styles which cut the body in two – although trench coats can be belted loosely at the back to keep a streamlined look at the front. Neutral colours (black, grey, stone, camel) are most versatile, although the new neutrals of olive, teal and aubergine are becoming increasingly popular. Remember that most raincoats are only shower-proof and in a torrential downpour will not protect your suit beneath unless you regularly treat the garment (especially after dry-cleaning) with a water-repellant spray.

Left: An overcoat is essential if you spend much time in cold climates; for warmer climates, or if you travel a lot by car, a rain/trench coat may be a better option (right).

Blazer/Sports Jacket

The most useful link-garment that a man can have in his wardrobe has to be a blazer or sports jacket, which possess almost chameleon-like powers when combined with different garments. A traditional navy blazer with metal buttons gives a very classic, traditional look when teamed with a shirt and tie and dark trousers. But when worn with light-coloured trousers, chinos or jeans, together with a sweater or T-shirt and loafers, its look is altogether more casual and relaxed. If a blazer is not appropriate for your personality or self-image, invest instead in a couple of quality sports jackets which give you far more choice in terms of fabric, cut and style. Cashmeres or meltons (a soft, fleecy fabric) come in a variety of different colours and give a more up-to-date look than the traditional navy blazer. Tweed gives a 'country gent' look, particularly when combined with brushed fabric trousers, a check shirt and knit tie. Checks and plaids can range from the very subtle to the very loud – subtle checks are the better choice for combining with patterned shirts or ties, and will give more flexibility in your wardrobe. Cotton or linen sports jackets are ideal for summer.

Fine Knitwear

A welcome alternative to the shirt and tie is a piece of fine-gauge knitwear worn with a suit or sports jacket. A cashmere turtle-neck sweater can look very smart and sophisticated, especially if the sweater is tucked into the trousers and finished off with a quality belt. Men with short necks should opt for a mock turtle-neck (which doesn't stand so high) or perhaps a fine-knit crew-neck sweater which gives even more space and freedom around the neck area and a slightly less austere look. Even V-neck sweaters are now being seen beneath formal suiting for a very modern, fashion-forward look.

Fine knitwear is also useful as a layering item. For example, a turtle-neck beneath a casual denim or lumberjack shirt adds warmth without extra bulk; and a V-neck or crew-neck sweater can look good over a T-shirt or casual shirt worn with chinos or jeans.

Above: Fine knitwear is an alternative to the shirt and tie and can be worn with a suit or sports jacket.

Polo-shirts

What began life as a garment for sportsmen has now become a staple of most men's wardrobes. The polo-shirt, once available only in white, now comes in a myriad of colours from palest pastels to deep, earthy shades and sharp, acid brights. In cotton, silk or wool, long-sleeved or short-sleeved, there are polo-shirts to suit all seasons and climates.

Worn with jeans, chinos or shorts they are ideal holiday or casual items, yet they can also be teamed with the smartest of suits for an unstuffy but semi-formal look. When left undone, the short row of buttons at the neck lends the wearer a more casual air, but when buttoned up completely to the collar the look becomes more formal and sophisticated.

Like fine-knits, polo-shirts are also good layering items. Try a T-shirt underneath and a V-neck sweater on top for a three-layered look.

Khakis/Chinos

Chinos and khaki pants have now officially replaced jeans as the favourite casual trouser in the male wardrobe. The reasons for this change of allegiance are probably comfort, versatility

Right: V-neck sweaters used only to be worn over shirts and ties during your school days, but today they are a fashion item in their own right.
Left: Polo-shirts, plain or patterned, and comfortable chinos have become basic wardrobe staples for men of all ages.
Far right: White crew-neck T-shirts and blue, denim jeans used to reign supreme as the kings of casual wear. Today there is such a wide range of T-shirt styles and casual pants that all men can develop an individual casual look to suit their shape, age and colouring.

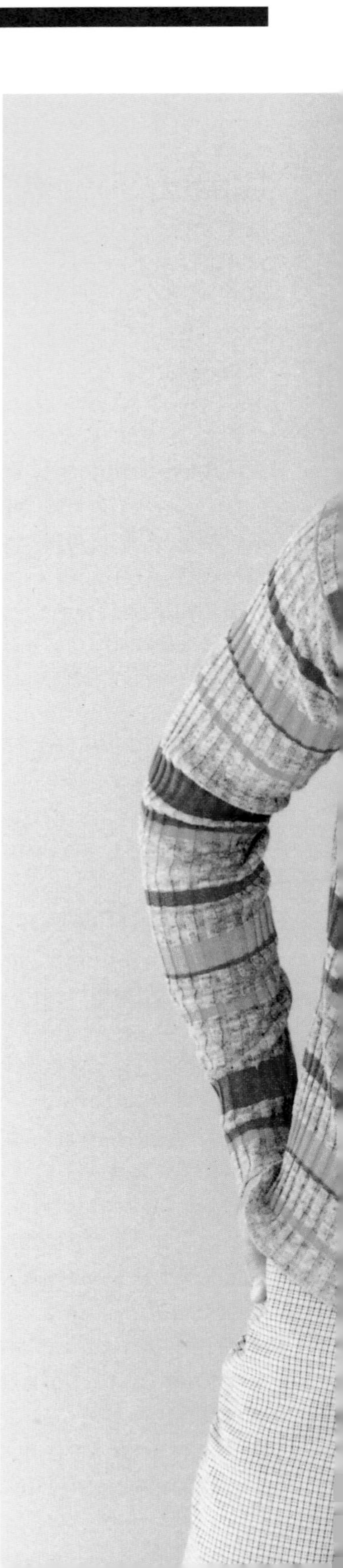

and aesthetics. Because they are made up in a cotton twill fabric chinos are more lightweight, easier to wash and cooler to wear than stiff, thick denim jeans. The cut of chinos is also much looser and baggier in the seat and thigh area, which makes them more comfortable than jeans. The range of colours makes them more versatile as a wardrobe item and, finally, the simplicity of the chino design (without too many pockets, seams and yokes) is very flattering – particularly to men with bigger than average bottoms or stomachs!

What began as a military garment available only in a neutral colour is now a basic wardrobe staple which can just as easily be worn to an office as to a beach or barbecue. Chinos are also the

one trouser which can take almost any kind of footwear – a formal laced-up brogue, loafer, boat-shoe, espadrille or sandal – and still look completely coordinated and stylish. Canvas belts look particularly good with chinos, but for a more formal look a plaited leather belt strikes just the right balance.

Jeans/Cargos/Carpenters

Although jeans may be losing their status as the No.1 casual item in men's wardrobes, as a fashion statement they are far from dead. Many designers and retailers are now reinventing the traditional jean in new fabrics and with innovative styling features to suit different tastes, ages and body shapes.

The traditional five-pocket western jean, as popularized by companies such as Levi, Lee and Wrangler, was originally only available in blue denim with a very straight cut, which was not flattering to all men. Today there are many variations on that theme, which include different colours (black is becoming increasingly popular as it looks slightly less casual), more relaxed cuts, stretch denim for comfort, and designs with fewer pockets and thinner seams for less bulk.

While in one direction jeans are becoming more classic, in another they are becoming more casual, with a slouchy, baggier cut and a proliferation of pockets, loops and zips. In these guises they are marketed as cargo pants and carpenter jeans, but the exaggerated styling lessens their versatility and marks them firmly as a casual item in the wardrobe in the way a classic pair is not.

Right: For men who don't like or suit T-shirts, the casual cotton shirt, plain or patterned, is the ideal companion for casual trousers and shorts or to dress-down a suit for an informal occasion.

T-shirts

This simple garment, which takes its name from its shape (a capital T), was originally an undergarment for sailors. It began to be worn as an outer garment in the rebellious years of the 1950s, when screen idols like James Dean daringly removed their shirts and wore sexy leather jackets over what was, essentially, their underwear. It has remained a wardrobe basic ever since and today is available in every colour imaginable, patterned or plain, with or without slogans and in a variety of different necklines.

The crew-neck is the original T-shirt neckline, but if you have a short or thick neck a V, square or football-neck (V-neck with collar) will be more flattering. The classic white T-shirt will take you anywhere and has become the uniform of men in the media, advertising and film world, who invariably sport it with a black jacket and the compulsory sunglasses. Men who are overweight, however, should remember that a white or horizontally striped T-shirt can be one of their worst enemies – deep coloured T-shirts with a loose, generous cut will be more flattering. Remember, also, that slogans on T-shirts act as horizontal lines.

Casual Shirts

Although T-shirts can look extremely good on lean, youthful figures, older or larger men may find the knit-jersey fabric too tight and clingy even in larger sizes. In this case a selection of loose shirts is a better option to achieve a casual look. For summer, look for short-sleeved shirts in plain, striped, geometric or floral cottons, depending on your tastes or the fashion trends of the moment. For winter, look for long-sleeved shirts in denim, fleecy fabrics, rough linen, moleskin, velour corduroy and knit-jersey.

Some casual winter shirts can double as lightweight jackets and can look good worn open with a crew-neck or polo-neck sweater or T-shirt beneath. For a very fashion-forward look, two coordinating shirts can even be worn together – one fastened and one left open. Banded-collar shirts (often called grandad shirts) can be worn buttoned-up with a suit, or left open beneath a sweater or waistcoat with jeans.

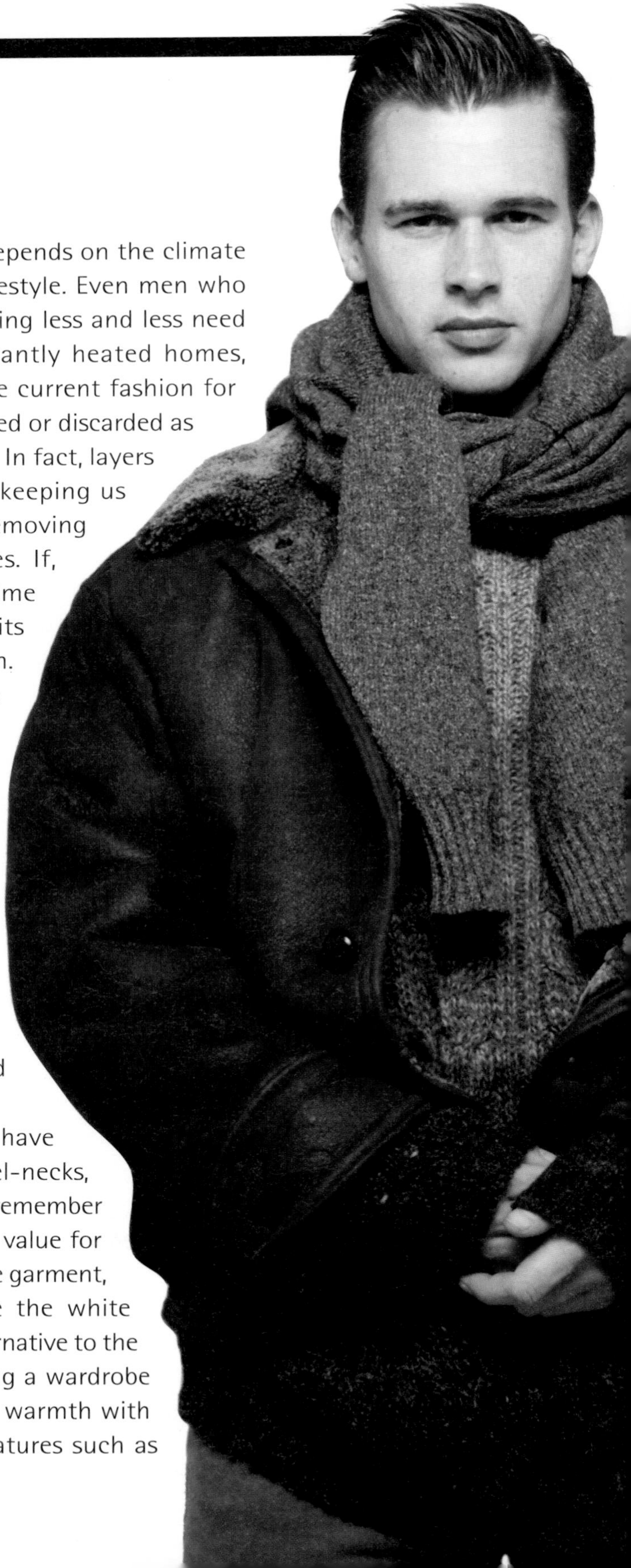

Chunky Knitwear

The necessity for bulky knitwear really depends on the climate in which you live and your particular lifestyle. Even men who live in colder climates, however, are finding less and less need for chunky knits because of our constantly heated homes, offices and modes of transport. Also, the current fashion for layering means that garments can be added or discarded as you go from one temperature to another. In fact, layers of thin garments are more efficient at keeping us warm than one thick garment – again, removing the need for lots of big, thick woollies. If, however, your lifestyle involves a lot of time spent outdoors in cold weather, bulky knits will need to be part of your wardrobe plan.

The most classic style to own is the Aran, which originated as a sweater for the fishermen of the Aran Islands off the west coast of Ireland. Made of coarse, off-white wool, it was traditionally hand-knitted in intricate cables, panels and bobbles. Cheaper, machine-knitted versions are available today in a variety of colours, including deep shades which are more flattering for larger men. If you prefer plainer sweaters, the oiled Guernsey sweaters are both flattering and hard-wearing.

More fashion-forward knits may have funnel-necks, cobweb-like stitches, bagel-necks, rolled hemlines or over-long sleeves. But remember when considering such sweaters that real value for money depends on how often you wear the garment, and these sweaters may easily become the white elephants of your wardrobe. A modern alternative to the chunky sweater which is rapidly becoming a wardrobe basic is the fleece, which combines great warmth with extreme lightness and more versatile features such as hoods, pockets and zip-fronts.

Casual Jackets

Going back not too many years, there was very little choice for men in the area of casual jackets – denim jeans jackets or leather bomber jackets for the young, car coats or anoraks for the older man. Today there is such a wealth of styles to choose from that a whole book could probably be written on this clothing alone.

Denim and leather jackets, car coats and anoraks are still part of the male fashion world, but you should be able to find several jackets for your wardrobe which are perfect for your body shape and lifestyle without having to compromise on style. In winter you can opt for the rugged outdoor look with a fur-hooded parka, shearling jacket, toggle-buttoned duffel-coat, checked blanket-jacket or navy reefer jacket. In summer there are probably even more styles to choose from – safari jackets, towelling-lined nylon cagoules, linen Nehru jackets, zip-front canvas jackets, shirt jackets, windcheaters, rubberized sailing jackets and multi-pocketed cargo jackets. For both seasons there are also lots of styles which have been borrowed from the active wear category to become everyday wardrobe basics – fleece jackets, body-warmers, sleeveless gilets, tracksuit-inspired jackets and hooded drawstring jackets.

Left: Chunky knits and thick casual jackets are a must if you spend time outdoors in the winter months. Otherwise, thinner knits, light fleeces and water-resistant jackets may be better options (right).

The Bottom Line: Socks and Shoes

Shoes and socks are such small items and yet the wrong styles or wrong sock/shoe combination can completely ruin your look. It is important that you possess the right footwear for the clothing items in your wardrobe and know which type of sock (or no sock at all) is best for each shoe. Research has shown that shoes are always noticed at interviews, and women in particular will invariably judge a man by his shoe and sock combination. Also, make sure your socks are long enough not to expose a hairy expanse of shin above the ankle when you sit down. Women have consistently voted this the least erogenous zone on a man – you have been warned!

Leather Lace-up Shoes

These are traditionally worn with suits and formal trousers and look best with a plain, dark sock or a subtly patterned one. White socks (unless you happen to be Michael Jackson or Brian Ferry) are a complete disaster, and jokey socks (like novelty ties) can seriously damage your credibility. Formal socks should be in wool or cotton to let your feet breathe – avoid all-nylon socks unless you want everyone else to avoid you.

Leather Slip-on Shoes or Loafers

These are a slightly less formal alternative to the lace-up shoe for suits and formal trousers, and the same sock guidelines apply when they are worn with these garments. Loafers can also look good with chinos and slacks, in which case a lighter sock colour can be worn (beige, stone, cream and so on) to match the shade of the trouser. When loafers are made in a very soft, supple leather (almost like slippers or moccasins) they can be worn with jeans or shorts, and socks can be abandoned altogether.

Sandals

This is the biggest problem for the average male. Socks or no socks? The answer lies in how much foot the sandal actually exposes – the more foot that is exposed, the less you can get away with wearing socks.

e-up shoes, slip-on fers, casual boots – make e you know what goes h what!

A very closed-in sandal can therefore be worn with a sock (of a similar colour to the sandal) and even with a lightweight summer suit such as cream linen. A sandal with only a few straps or a single strap (called a slide or mule) looks ridiculous with socks and needs completely bare feet and a very casual outfit – for instance jeans or shorts. Hiking sandals with broad nylon or leather straps and lots of velcro fastenings are excellent for walking and rough terrain. These should never be worn with socks as the base of the sandal is moulded to the shape of the foot for better grip – they look great with cargo pants, carpenter jeans or bush shorts. Coloured, plastic or rubber sandals or flip-flops are best saved for the beach, worn with swimwear or brightly coloured shorts.

Boots

These range from smart lace-up or elasticated-side formal styles, through light-coloured suede boots, to thick-soled hiking or construction-site footwear. The more formal styles can be worn with suits for a fashion-forward look and need plain, long, dark socks. Suede boots (which vary from ankle- to calf-length) look good with jeans or chinos and need a thick, ribbed cotton sock. Hiking or construction-style boots (including the now classic Doc Martens) need a thick, chunky woollen sock and an informal trouser such as jeans, cargos or carpenters.

Trainers

After starting life as a sports shoe for track and field events trainers have now become the one shoe throughout the world which almost every man, woman and child owns regardless of whether they have ever done a day's exercise in their life. Even though they are worn as an everyday item and come in a myriad of different styles, colours and fabrics, they still look their best with toweling sports socks and casual garments – jeans, sweat-pants, track suits or shorts. Suede or canvas trainers in dark colours (navy, black, burgundy) have a slightly less casual look and can be teamed with smarter garments for a semi-casual look.

Boat/Deck Shoes

These are gaining in popularity in many men's wardrobes,

probably because chinos and khakis are replacing jeans as the most popular form of casual wear. Boat shoes (leather) and deck shoes (canvas) are ideal companions to chinos, slacks and khakis, and can be worn with socks in winter and without in summer. If either type of shoe is to be worn without socks, make sure you buy the styles with ventilation holes in the side to allow your feet to breathe in hot weather.

Accessories may be just small finishing touches but they can contribute immensely to your image.

Breaking the Rules

Just as you can mix casual garments with formal garments to achieve an individual or trendy look, you can, of course, break the shoe/sock rules for similar effects. So, yes, you can wear trainers with a suit; Doc Martens with shorts or socks with strappy sandals – but remember, not everyone will get the joke!

The Final Touch: Accessories

Like socks and shoes, accessories can be quite small items which speak volumes in very loud words. Mobile phones which play little tunes, watches with bright plastic straps, battered brief-cases or gold medallions all send out messages about the type of person you are. So have a good look at all the finishing touches to your appearance and judge the impact they are making – for better or worse!

Rings and Things

When it comes to jewellery on a man, the general consensus is 'less is more' – in other words, less is definitely more stylish. Obviously, attitudes to jewellery can differ from profession to profession – earrings are practically compulsory in some arty professions but actually banned in ultra-conservative workplaces. An interesting ring (together with a wedding ring) can be an acceptable accessory, but by far the most stylish and acceptable items of jewellery that a man can wear are cufflinks.

Like ties, cufflinks allow a man to express a degree of individuality and personality when wearing a formal outfit, and their quality and style are always noticed by others. (Like jokey socks and ties, novelty cufflinks are best kept for family occasions where everyone knows you and impressions don't matter!) If your

cufflinks are coloured, it looks more stylish if the colours are related to the pattern in your tie – with plain silver or gold cufflinks, a connection to the metal of your watch looks most harmonious.

Neck chains and bracelets can cheapen a formal look and are best reserved for casual occasions.

Watches and Phones

In the past a watch was a huge investment; a man possessed only one during his lifetime, and usually passed it on to the next generation as a family heirloom.

But with today's new technologies and lower prices it is entirely possible for a man to own several watches, and this is advisable if you have a varied lifestyle.

For business, non-digital, discreet watches are most stylish with a plain leather, mock-crocodile or metal strap. Chunky, sporty or plastic varieties are best kept for casual or leisure occasions unless your profession is a very relaxed or fashion-conscious one. Ornate, diamond-encrusted watches, like too much jewellery, can look ostentatious and are best reserved for evening occasions.

Mobile phones have become a common accessory, and they too can be adapted to different occasions. Choose brightly coloured snap-on faces for casual/leisure days and darker or more discreet panels or leather cases for the workplace. Do make sure that you choose a subtle ringing-tone – nothing is more irritating to others than high-pitched jingles.

Look the Business

Nothing lets a businessman down more than an old, broken briefcase, scrappy pads of paper and a plastic ballpoint pen. Just as your make and style of car conveys status and authority, a quality pen, good leather briefcase (boxy, combination-lock styles are now definitely passé) an electronic organizer, lap-top or filofax will send signals of professionalism and credibility. In more relaxed or creative professions, a quality leather back-pack is an acceptable alternative to a briefcase, and is especially useful if you travel frequently on business.

Chapter
8

New Directions

Blokes Don't Do Makeovers

To put all the theories into practice, I sent out a message via my friends, family and colleagues to find a good selection of men – all shapes, sizes, ages and colour patterns – to be my makeover stars for a day. One of these brave souls just happened to be a journalist (I hoped this wouldn't backfire on me!) who later described his makeover experience for his newspaper's readers. You can see Graham's makeover results on page 148 but first let him explain in his own words the delights of a day of pampering...

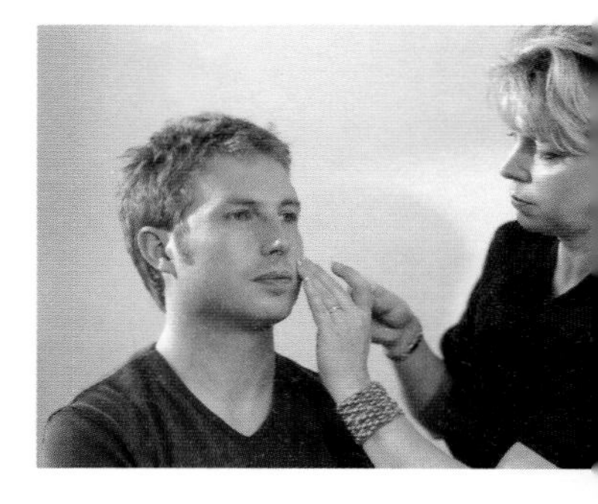

Graham tries hard to look like he's *not* enjoying himself . . .

❝ BLOKES don't do makeovers. Just like blokes don't do pyjama parties, beauty therapy or lip gloss. So why then was I sitting in a chair having my hair coiffured and my colours analysed? 'It's becoming far more acceptable with men these days', assured Carol Spenser as she smeared green paste on my face to "smooth out the red bits". And in a way she was quite right. I remember my mother almost pinning my dad down just to put a bit of moisturiser on his weather beaten face, but these days it's as normal as under-arm deodorant. The times they are a changin', and if Carol is right, before long every flush faced, red blooded man won't leave the bathroom without a smear of green cream.

I really didn't know what to expect when my hairdresser Paul Falltrick called to tell me I was the 'only redhead we can think of', and to 'expect a call telling you what to do on the day of the shoot' before hanging up. Terror rose within me. Had he told them what I look like? I might have the right hair (more an autumn shade of leaf as my friend would call it), but I was positive I wasn't model material. Absolutely positive. But the day came, and to be honest, I was flattered.

Now I was sitting in a make-up chair with a can of lager in front of me to 'make you relax in front of the camera', and six pairs of eyes watching the bags under my eyes being concealed. 'It won't show', confided Carol in a reassuring tone, before applying clear mascara to my eyelashes. Of course it showed. The mascara had crossed the boundaries of what a man can reasonably accept.

The girls were expecting me out there in front of the cameras, stamping my mark in the *Style Directions for Men* book, and quite frankly there was no backing down. In a biscuit coloured linen suit and chocolate brown V-neck T-shirt I struck my poses, to claps and cheers from Tony the photographer and an array of females I couldn't see – because my new look was minus my glasses.

So here I was, in a plush Islington studio with a world-class hairdresser, a make-up artist, author, various other necessary people and a photographer snapping my every move, while trying to look like I wasn't enjoying myself. I couldn't, because I was a man and men don't do makeovers.

But the fact is everyone, without exception, loves being pampered, and you show me a man who won't enjoy half a dozen gorgeous women telling him how good he looks, and I will show you a liar. I felt like the centre of the universe, wise-cracks fell from my mouth like biscuit crumbs, this was wonderful.

Right then, I'm ready for my manicure ... !”

Bal Walter Paul Rick Carol Graham Ian Brad Adam and Michael

Makeover 1– Rick

Name: Rick Attlesey **Age:** Late 30s
Occupation: Builder
Face Direction: Round with mainly soft features
Body Direction: Contoured
Colour Direction: Bright (brown hair, green eyes, fair skin)
Needs: To smarten up his look for a forthcoming black-tie event at his wife's work place

STYLE DIRECTIONS

Clothes

Rick arrived in his builder's gear – complete with muddy boots and hard hat! A transformation from this extreme state may seem easy, but achieving a flattering evening look for a stocky man like Rick needs careful consideration. Because of his Contoured bodyshape, he definitely needs a single-breasted jacket with a rounded hemline and his soft face needs a notched, rather than peaked lapel. A bow-tie is a must for this look but Rick should avoid up-turned wing collars because of his short neck and opt for a turned-down spread collar. A cummerbund would only put a horizontal line around his stomach and add to its width, so Rick is best to leave the pleats of his dress-shirt on show to elongate his torso – a waistcoat would also be flattering. Rick's Bright colouring can take the stark contrast of black and white extremely well – he can even wear a bright bow-tie or waistcoat and not look 'overpowered' by the intensity of colour.

Grooming Directions

Rick's naturally curly hair had grown into quite a rounded shape, which together with his full beard only emphasised and widened his round face. Paul Falltrick cut his hair much closer at the sides of his face and removed the side parts of his beard to create 'vertical' lines which slim and elongates the face.

Makeover 2 – Adam

Name: Adam Docker **Age:** Late 20s
Occupation: TV and Video Cameraman
Face Direction: Square with mainly angular features
Body Direction: Triangular
Colour Direction: Muted (light brown hair, hazel eyes, tanned skin)
Needs: To try a more contemporary casual look as a change from jeans and T-shirts

STYLE DIRECTIONS

Clothes

Adam's physique (ideal for balancing a heavy camera on your shoulders all day!) is perfect for the jeans and T-shirt look which is always most flattering on men whose waist and hips are smaller than their shoulders. A more contemporary casual look, however, is cargo pants with bellow-pockets (which need slim thighs) and a zip-front gilet with a T-shirt beneath. Adam's angular face is complemented by the sharp lines of the up-turned collar on the gilet and the V-neck of the T-shirt. As he does have slim thighs, he can also take the gilet ending at wrist-length and, as he has a long neck, it could be zipped right to the chin and still be flattering. The subtle shades of slate grey and petrol blue are well suited to Adam's sultry, Muted colouring.

Grooming Directions

As Adam's face is quite square, Paul took away a lot of the bulk of his hair at the sides and styled it back from the face to show off his wonderful cheekbones! Some blonde highlights were added to sections of Adam's hair at the front which worked well with his hazel eyes and tanned skin. Finally, a finishing wax was applied – especially to the ends of the hair – for extra definition and control.

Makeover 3 – Michael

Name: Michael White **Age:** Mid 50s
Occupation: Financial Advisor
Face Direction: Rectangular with mainly angular features
Body Direction: Rectangular
Colour Direction: Cool (silver grey hair, brown eyes, medium skin tone)
Needs: To achieve a more relaxed and current look for his hair and clothing

STYLE DIRECTIONS

Clothes

Michael's wardrobe consists mainly of suits, shirts and ties – which presents problems for weekends and holidays. Being tall and slim with a Straight bodyshape, he would suit the classic jeans and T-shirt look but to give more flexibility in his wardrobe and more opportunity to create a smart-casual look, I suggested he incorporate a range of neutral-coloured chinos, colourful polo-shirts or casual shirts, a couple of casual jackets and a few pairs of loafer-style shoes. The neutral-coloured chinos and navy, zip-front, blouson-style jacket will mix and match with lots of different colours and the bright turquoise polo-shirt is ideal for Michael's Cool colouring.

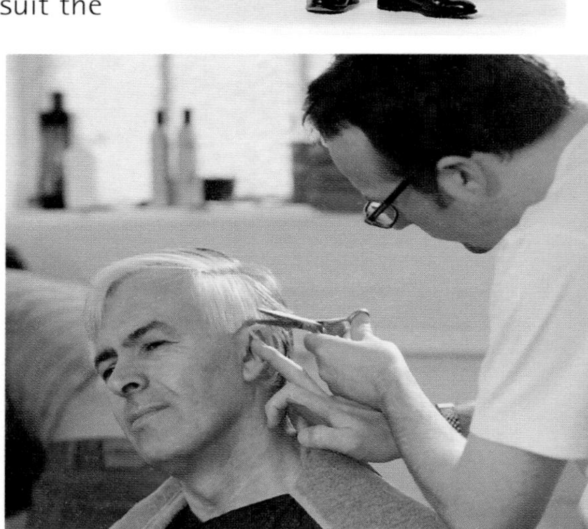

Grooming Directions

As Michael had worn his hair in the same side-parted, one length style for many years, it definitely had to go! Paul layered the hair all over and styled it forward onto the forehead with a short, choppy fringe which suits his rectangular face and gives a much younger look. Paul also recommended that Michael use a blue/violet-coloured shampoo specially formulated to remove all yellow traces from his silver-grey hair.

Makeover 4 – Graham

Name: Graham Hutson **Age:** Late 20s
Occupation: Journalist
Face Direction: Oval with mainly angular features
Body Direction: Rectangular
Colour Direction: Warm (red hair, green eyes, fair/freckled skin)
Needs: To try a suit (because he doesn't possess one) without looking stuffy

STYLE DIRECTIONS

Clothes

Graham arrived dressed in totally cool-toned colours – greys and blues – which, together with black, are his usual choice. He looked a bit aghast when I suggested he try browns and beiges but he did confess at the end that when wearing these he looked less pale and drained. The biscuit-coloured, single-breasted suit gave a relaxed, un-stuffy look because of its fabric (linen) and the fact that we teamed it with a casual V-neck T-shirt. Graham's glasses were whisked off because they were a bit too cool for his warm colouring – gold, squares or rectangles look fantastic for both glasses and sunglasses.

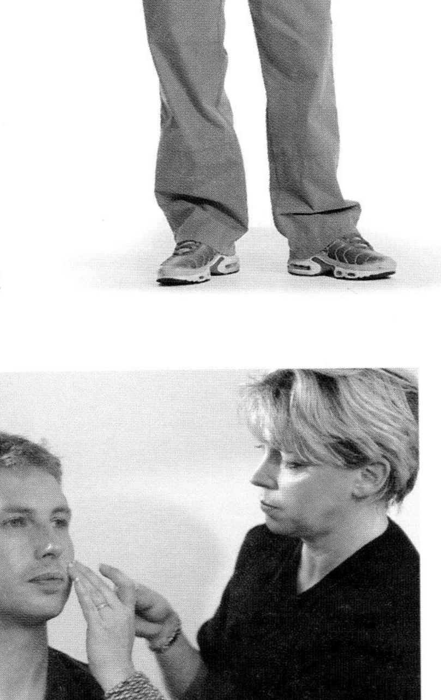

Grooming Directions

Like many red-heads, Graham has a naturally ruddy complexion which can make others think he is blushing all the time! The remedy is a simple green-tinted moisturiser which, because green is the opposite colour to red in the spectrum, counteracts the redness to leave the skin a natural beige tone. (Graham can rest assured that the green cream was also used on most of the other men – either for red cheeks, red noses or to counteract shaving redness!) Although Graham's hair was quite short, Paul took it even shorter to lose its rounded shape and styled it into a more spiky look with small amounts of moulding wax.

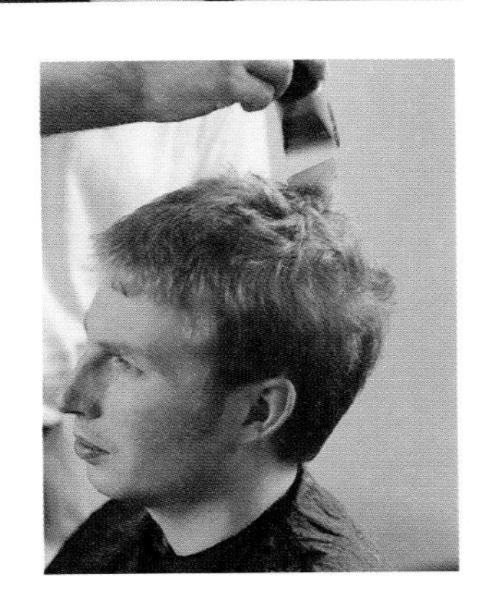

Makeover 5 – Brad

Name: Brad Wray **Age:** Mid 40s
Occupation: Headmaster
Face Direction: Oval with mostly soft features
Body Directions: Contoured
Colour Direction: Deep (dark hair, brown eyes, olive skin tone)
Needs: To find his best style of suit for work – smart, authoritative and fashionable!

STYLE DIRECTIONS

Clothes

Being a headmaster, Brad has a difficult balancing act to perform as he needs to look 'in control' but also 'in touch' with current attitudes. His way of achieving this has been to aim for a semi-smart look with a navy blazer, shirt and tie and light coloured chinos. This is not his best look as he is not very tall and the two blocks of colour shorten and widen his body. Neither is a double-breasted blazer the best choice for a Contoured bodyshape, and the turn-ups on the chinos only serve to shorten his legs still further, His best option is a single-breasted suit – curved hemline and no vents to the jacket and no turn-ups on the trousers – combined with a current look in shirts and ties. For the shoot we chose a black shirt with fashionable grey/silver tie. Brad had never considered a charcoal suit before or a dark shirt with lighter tie but really liked the resulting combination. What will the children think of his new image?

Grooming Directions

As Brad has very little hair on his head, he has done the sensible thing and kept it very short. Paul took it *even* shorter still (to an almost 'shaven-headed' look) which always gives an air of strength and confidence. A beard with this image, however, can make the face look unbalanced (almost upside-down!) so Brad decided to take the plunge and shave it all off. With a fantastic olive skin tone all that was needed for the final finishing touch was a dab of powder on the top of his head to take the shine off for the photos!

Makeover 6 – Bal

Name: Bal Sanghera **Age:** Mid 30s
Occupation: Financial controller for a magazine publisher
Face Directions: Rectangular with mainly angular features
Body Direction: Triangular
Colour Direction: Deep (black hair, brown eyes, dark skin)
Needs: To add new colours to his wardrobe as a change from endless black

STYLE DIRECTIONS

Clothes

Bal does not have to wear a suit to his office as the atmosphere is quite relaxed and informal. His normal look is black trousers or jeans with a loose shirt or T-shirt - usually also in black or occasionally in grey. Having Deep as his Primary Colour Direction, Bal definitely suits black near the face but a pale grey shirt is not a great choice unless it is combined with a deeper jacket. To give Bal a slightly smarter look I chose a bright lime polo-shirt with a black stripe on the collar and sleeves – most 'Bright' colours will suit him as they usually have 'Deep' as their secondary Colour Direction. As Bal has a Triangular bodyshape he can tuck the polo-shirt into his trousers and define his waistline with an eye-catching belt which also has the effect of accentuating his broad shoulders.

Grooming Directions

Bal normally ties his shoulder-length hair back for work but his long, rectangular face needs some width of hair to balance its proportions. Paul cut a little off the ends to create a wide wedge-shape and make sure his hair cleared the shoulder-line. Bal's naturally curly hair was dried with a diffuser on the hairdryer to prevent frizziness and then sprayed with a finishing gel to define the curls and create a healthy shine.

MAINE

Makeover 7 – Walter

Name: Walter Merriman **Age:** Late 60s
Occupation: Retired
Face Direction: Rectangular with mainly angular features
Body Direction: Rectangular
Colour Direction: Cool (grey hair, blue eyes, medium skin tone)
Needs: To develop a smarter casual look for his retired lifestyle

STYLE DIRECTIONS

Clothes

Although Walter has been retired for several years and now leads a more leisurely lifestyle, he cannot rid himself of the 'shirt and tie' habit acquired from a lifetime working in an engineering office. His attempt to look more casual was to combine his formal jacket shirt and tie with roomy trousers, a cardigan and trainers. The result is a mixture of far too many different patterns, colours and textures – red and grey diagonals on the tie; burgundy and brown horizontals on the cardigan; and black and grey tweedy flecks on the jacket. Also, as the eye is always drawn to the brightest part of an outfit, the eye is grabbed by the white trainers making them the focal point of the outfit. After Walter's makeover the red polo-shirt (buttoned up to the neck as Walter has a long neck and angular face) now grabs the attention and is perfect for his Cool Colouring. The vertical stripes on the navy, knitted waistcoat accentuate his slim, rectangular bodyshape and he is tall enough (6'4") to take a cropped, blouson jacket and turn-ups on his trousers. The trainers were banished in favour of black slip-on shoes – his wife was very pleased!

Grooming Directions

Walter's medium skin tone had no visible redness although he was advised to switch from aftershave lotion to a moisturising balm as his skin was quite dry in places. His hair was also quite dry so after deep conditioning the damaged ends were removed and the hair was styled much closer to his head with a little gel resulting in a suave, elegant look.

Makeover 8 – Ian

Name: Ian Howarth **Age:** Early 20s
Occupation: Insurance Consultant
Face Direction: Rectangular with mainly angular features
Body Direction: Triangular
Colour Direction: Bright (dark brown hair, blue eyes, fair skin tone)
Needs: To smarten up his look to begin a new job the following week!

STYLE DIRECTIONS

Clothes

As Ian had just secured his first job in the insurance industry he needed a complete change of image – from student to city executive – to give prospective clients confidence in his knowledge and abilities! Hidden beneath a straggly hairstyle and baggy shirt was a fine chiselled face, an athletic bodyshape (he plays lots of football) and very Bright colouring (he is of Irish decent). Although his Triangular bodyshape could take a double-breasted suit, this look was too 'old' for him, so a high-closure, straight-hemmed, vented single-breasted style was chosen with double-pleated trousers and a quality belt. The contrast in his colouring (pale skin, dark hair, blue eyes) could easily take the brightness of the purple shirt and tie without him looking overpowered. A pair of modern, side-buckled shoes completed his new 'successful executive' image.

Grooming Directions

Although Ian's girlfriend was not too keen, Paul Falltrick wanted to give Ian a really short, designer hairstyle to complement his new designer suit. After taking off most of the length, the ends of the hair were razored into a sharp, uneven style which was further enhanced by twisting the sections of the hair with wax into a choppy style. Ian's most painful moment of the day was when I plucked away the hairs from the bridge of his nose to give him two eyebrows instead of one!

Personal Style Directions for Women

Why not treat the woman in your life to an exclusive mail-order-makeover pack or a signed style book direct from Carol Spenser's office?

For just £29.95, the Personal Style Directions pack provides a personalised face and figure analysis, colour and make-up advice, a wardrobe guide and current fashion information. Join the exclusive group who have benefited from Carol's advice via her TV and magazine makeovers with this unique Personal Style Directions makeover pack.

How to Apply

To receive your Personal Style Directions pack, simply fill in a questionnaire giving details of your physical characteristics, colouring, bodyshape, figure proportions etc. You also need to send two recent photographs: a head-and-shoulders shot (to check your colouring/face shape/glasses etc.) and a full-length shot (to check your figure, proportions etc.). Your application form and photographs are analysed by Carol Spenser and her trained staff, who then produce your Personal Style Directions pack.

Your Personal Style Directions Pack will contain:

- Face Directions – suggestions for hairstyles, glasses, jewellery
- Figure Directions – guidelines for your best clothing shapes
- Proportional Problems – solved with easy-to-follow tips
- Colour Directions – perfect shades for your clothes and make-up
- Wardrobe Directions – to suit your shape and lifestyle
- Fashion Directions – over 50 pages of the latest fashions
- Colour Directions Wallet – a handy reminder of 'near face' colours
- Quality Lipstick – selected for your Colour direction

At only £29.95 Personal Style Directions is approximately one third the price of a full style consultation – so don't delay! Return the slip on page 160 to receive your application form.

Visit Our Website!

www.styledirections.com

- features
- advice
- products
- on-line ordering

Special Book Offers

As a valued purchaser of *Style Directions for Men*, you can receive Carol Spenser's other popular books at a reduced price direct from her office. Your books can also be signed by Carol on special request – if a personal message is required, please print it clearly on plain paper and attach it to the application form on page 160.

Style Directions for Women

A companion book to *Style Directions for Men* (published Oct '99), this indispensable book gives women in-depth information on how to develop their best personal style. This 160 page book, packed with colour photos and illustrations, shows how to plan a versatile wardrobe, how to follow fashion each season; how to accessorise – plus lots more on figure problems, hairstyles, Colour Directions and skin care and make-up routines.
Hardback price £15.99 (inc p+p) Normal price £17.99 - save £2.00
Paperback price £11.99 (inc p+p) Normal price £12.99 - Save £1.00

Wedding Style Counsel

Carol Spenser's second book (published July '96) is an indispensable read for every bride-to-be. Chapter by chapter, the book helps with every big decision of style – the wedding dress, headdress, flowers, lingerie, cosmetics, groom and attendants' outfits – plus guidelines for suits and hats for civil weddings, going away outfits and mothers of the bride and groom. This 160 page book, packed with colour photos, guarantees a stylish and perfectly co-ordinated wedding whatever your budget.
Price **£12.99** (inc p+p) normal price £15.99 – save £3.00

Petite Style Counsel

Carol Spenser's third book (published May '98) provides excellent style advice for all women under 5'4" – who now account for 42% of the UK female population. Packed full of invaluable hints and tips on how to look (and feel!) an extra few inches taller, this book covers all aspects of style from hairstyles and handbags to swimsuits and sarongs. A big buy for little women!
Price **£4.99** (inc p+p) Normal price £5.99 – save £1.00

Slimline Style Counsel

Carol Spenser's fourth book (published May '98) shows you how to look slimmer without going on a crash diet! The average dress size in the UK is now size 16 and the average cup size of a bra is now a D-cup. The female figure has changed from the 'hour-glass' of the 40s and 50s to a straighter, stronger shape that needs a new style of dressing. Learn how to flatter your figure whether you're a size 14 or 24.
Price **£4.99** (inc p+p) Normal price £5.99 – save £1.00

Order form

Cut out or photocopy this form and send to:
Style Directions
Mendham Watermill, Mill Lane, Mendham, Harleston, IP20 0NN.

Name ....

Address ....

....

....

Post code ....

Tel No. ....

Please send me (tick boxes)

❑ **Personal Style Directions pack**
pack for women - £29.95

❑ **Style Directions for Women**
Price £15.99 hbk ❑ £11.99 pbk ❑

❑ **Wedding Style Counsel**
Price £12.99

❑ **Petite Style Counsel**
Price £4.99

❑ **Slimline Style Counsel**
Price £4.99

❑ Details of Style and Colour Courses
Free

Total amount £______

❑ I enclose a cheque*

❑ I wish to pay by Access/Visa/Mastercard

No | | | | | | | | | | | | | | | | |

Expires end ....

Signature ....

* Please make cheques payable to Style Directions

Products and Services

A wide range of products and services are available to the general public, image and colour consultants, and members of the fashion and beauty industries. These include Colour Directions swatch cards and wallets, Colour Directions capes, a quality range of Colour Cosmetics and current or back orders of the Fashion Directions booklets. Discounts are available for bulk orders on some products, and customers can be added to our credit-card mailing list to receive the Fashion Directions booklet on a twice yearly basis. Visit our website: www.styledirections.com to view our range of products.

Style and Colour Courses

If you would like to experience 'hands-on' advice from Carol Spenser or her team of trained consultants, 3-day style and colour workshops or week-long courses are available. You may want to treat yourself, you may be considering starting your own business or you may simply want to add an extra service to your existing business. Whatever your reason, certification from the UK's leading style company gives you a flying start.

Business Directions Seminars or personal consultations can be tailored to the specific needs of individual companies to ensure that all personnel, (male and female), are making the right impact. Special training programmes in the areas of Colour Directions and Personal Shopping can be devised for fashion and beauty retailers, and makeovers or personal consultations can be arranged as incentives or promotions for staff and customers.

For further information, please contact:
Style Directions,
Mendham Watermill, Mill Lane, Mendham, Harleston, IP20 0NN.
Tel: 01379 855410 Fax: 01379 855414
email: publicpersona@dial.pipex.com
Website: www. styledirections.com